The New Zealand Medal 1845-47 and 1860-66

compiled and edited by W. H. Feyver and J. W. Wilson

The roll for the New Zealand Medal 1845-47 and 1860-66 which follows is transcribed from the Admiralty records which reside at the Public Record Office (ADM171-16) and are reproduced here with the permission of the Controller of HM Stationery Office.

The recipients of the medals are listed under a heading showing the ship's name, a date (see comments below) and some reference to those eligible for the award.

The dates referred to above take the form of 1845-47, 1860-63, etc and in some cases these correspond with the dates found on the reverse of the medals. However, there are *known examples* of medals where the dates on the reverse do not match the dates which appear at the beginning of each ship's list of medal recipients. The reasons for this are not clear but the problem could well form an interesting research project.

We draw no conclusions from these differences in dates other than emphasising that the dates we quote are those on the medal rolls.

The casualty details recorded in the following text are taken from a list of seventy casualties currently held at the Ministry of Defence, and reproduced here with their permission. Of these, only twenty-nine subsequently claimed their medals. It should be noted that only survivors could claim their medals.

LIST OF SHIPS AND MEDAL ENTITLEMENT

1845-1847

Ships		No. of Medals issued
H.M.S.	Calliope	62
H.M.S.	Castor	69
H.M.S.	Driver	10
H.E.I.C.S.	Elphinstone	6
H.M.S.	Hazard	35
H.M.S.	Inflexible	20
H.M.S.	North Star	41
H.M.S.	Osprey	11
H.M.S.	Racehorse	36
Sub Total		290

1860-1866

Ships		No. of Medals issued
H.M.S.	Brisk	13
H.M.S.	Cordelia	29
H.M.S.	Curacoa	187
H.M.S.	Eclipse	75
H.M.S.	Esk	119
H.M.S.	Falcon	12
H.M.S.	Harrier	80
H.M.S.	Himalaya	1
H.M.S.	Iris	72
H.M.S.	Miranda	91
H.M.S.	Niger	66
H.M.S.	Pelorus	117
H.M.C.S.	Victoria	40
Sub Total		902
Total		1192

CASUALTIES 1860–1866

The following casualties have been abstracted from official government records presently held by the Ministry of Defence. They are contained in a volume which covers the period 1854–1909. Casualties for the New Zealand War of 1845–1847 were not available from this source.

Note: In the following rolls (*) indicates duplicate medal issued. Casualties are indicated by **bold** type.

Name	Rank	Ship	Place	Casualty Details Date	Type of Injury
Alexander, H. McC.	Lieut	*Curacoa*	Rangariri	20.11.63	Wounded	Gunshot – scalp & axilla
Allison, W.	L Seaman	*Esk*	Tepapa	29.04.64	Wounded	Gunshot – chest & thigh
Alton, G.	Gunr (RMA)	*Miranda*	Tepapa	29.04.64	Wounded	Gunshot – right thigh
Andrews, G.	AB	*Miranda*	Rangariri	20.11.63	Wounded	Cutlass – right leg
Barrett, C.	Ord	*Harrier*	Tepapa	29.04.64	Wounded	Gunshot – left thigh
Blake, W. H.	Lieut	*Niger*	Omata	28.03.60	Wounded	Wound – right breast
Bowden, A.	AB	*Esk*	Tepapa	29.04.64	Wounded	Gunshot – right heel
Bryan, M.	AB	*Miranda*	Tepapa	29.04.64	Wounded	Gunshot – left leg
Burchill, W.	Ord	*Harrier*	Tepapa	29.04.64	Wounded	Gunshot – right hip
Claringbold, G.	L Seaman	*Miranda*	Tepapa	29.04.64	Wounded	Gunshot – left leg
Clark, W.	Pte	*Niger*	Omata	28.03.60	Wounded	Wound – knee
Clarke, H.	Boy	*Harrier*	Tepapa	29.04.64	**Killed**	Gunshot – neck
Corker, G.	Cpl	*Eclipse*	Opotiki	22.05.65	Wounded	Gunshot – left arm
Dalton, W.	Qtrmstr	*Esk*	Tepapa	29.04.64	**Killed**	Gunshot – lung & head
Dollar, T.	AB	*Curacoa*	Rangariri	20.11.63	Wounded	Gunshot – right shoulder
Donnelly, T.	Ord	*Esk*	Tepapa	29.04.64	Wounded	Sprain – leg
Downer, P.	Pte	*Harrier*	Rangariri	20.11.63	**Killed**	Gunshot – chest
Downes, E. D. P.	Lieut	*Miranda*	Rangariri	20.11.63	Wounded	Gunshot – right shoulder
Duff, G. G.	Lieut	*Esk*	Tepapa	29.04.64	Wounded	(Gunshot – back (Bayonet – thigh
English, J.	Capt M'top	*Miranda*	Tepapa	29.04.64	Wounded	Gunshot – left thigh
Fox, W.	AB	*Curacoa*	Tepapa	29.04.64	Wounded	Gunshot – foot
Foyer, W.	Bombdr	*Esk*	Tepapa	29.04.64	Wounded	Gunshot – left arm
Fuller, R.	Ord	*Esk*	Tepapa	29.04.64	**Killed**	Gunshot – head
Galling, T.	L Seaman	*Miranda*	Rangariri	20.11.63	Wounded	Gunshot – right leg
Glanville, R.	Capt F'top	*Niger*	Omata	28.03.60	Wounded	Wound – leg
Greenhorn, A.	Stoker	*Harrier*	Tepapa	29.04.64	**Killed**	(Gunshot – abdomen (Tomahawk – abdomen
Hamilton, J. F. C.	Captain	*Esk*	Tepapa	29.04.64	**Killed**	Gunshot – head
Hammick, R. F.	Lieut	*Miranda*	Tepapa	29.04.64	Wounded	Gunshot – right shoulder
Harding, H. J.	Sergt	*Eclipse*	Tepapa	29.04.64	**Killed**	Gunshot – mouth & chest
Harris, J.	Ord	*Curacoa*	Tepapa	29.04.64	**Killed**	Gunshot – head
Hay, E. W.	Comdr	*Harrier*	Tepapa	29.04.64	**Died/Wounds**	Gunshot – abdomen (died 30.04.64)
Hayles, S.	Ord	*Curacoa*	Rangariri	20.11.63	Wounded	Gunshot – right thigh
Hill, C.	Lieut	*Curacoa*	Tepapa	29.04.64	**Killed**	Gunshot – head (twice)
Holland, G.	AB	*Curacoa*	Tama	12.08.65	**Killed**	Gunshot – stomach
Hotham, C. F.	Lieut	*Curacoa*	Rangariri	20.11.63	Wounded	Gunshot – right leg
Jeffery, R.	AB	*Esk*	Tepapa	29.04.64	Wounded	Sprain – leg
Joyce, W.	Bombdr	*Esk*	Tepapa	29.04.64	Wounded	Gunshot – arm
Kent, L.	Bosn Mte	*Miranda*	Tepapa	29.04.64	**Died/Wounds**	Gunshot – left thigh
Knight, J.	Capt F'cle	*Esk*	Tepapa	29.04.64	Wounded	Gunshot – right shoulder
Lawrence, J.	AB	*Esk*	Tepapa	29.04.64	Wounded	Wound – scalp
Leigh, W.	Stoker	*Esk*	Tepapa	29.04.64	**Killed**	(Gunshot – head (Tomahawk – fractured skull
Lockie, A.	AB	*Harrier*	Tepapa	29.04.64	Wounded	Gunshot – right elbow
McAlister, A.	AB	*Miranda*	Tepapa	29.04.64	Wounded	Gunshot – arm
Martin, E.	AB	*Esk*	Tepapa	29.04.64	Wounded	Gunshot – hip & loins
Mayne, R. C.	Comdr	*Eclipse*	Rangariri	20.11.63	Wounded	Gunshot – left hip

Name	Rank	Ship	Place	Casualty Details Date	Type of Injury
Millard, T.	Bosn Mte	*Niger*	Omata	28.03.60	Wounded Wound – head
Mitchell, W. E.	Lieut	*Esk*	R. Waipia	03.02.64	Died/Wounds Gunshot – chest
Noakes, J.	Bosn Mte	*Miranda*	Tepapa	29.04.64	Wounded Gunshot – left shoulder
Oldfield, H.	AB	*Eclipse*	Rangariri	20.11.63	Wounded Gunshot – left shoulder, left arm & knee
Osborne, F.	Capt M'top	*Harrier*	Rangariri	20.11.63	Killed Gunshot – neck
Palmer, W.	Pte	*Niger*	Omata	28.03.60	Wounded Wound – knee
Pallatt, J.	L Seaman	*Harrier*	Tepapa	29.04.64	Wounded Gunshot – finger
Parker, P. R. H.	Sub Lieut	*Falcon*	Tepapa	29.04.64	Wounded Gunshot – abdomen
Roberts, T.	AB	*Esk*	Tepapa	29.04.64	Wounded Gunshot – abdomen
Robinson, W.	AB	*Curacoa*	Rangariri	20.11.63	Wounded Gunshot – left leg
Ruthven, S.	AB	*Miranda*	Tepapa	29.04.64	Wounded Gunshot – left lung and fractured arm
Smith, A.	L Seaman	*Curacoa*	Tepapa	29.04.64	Wound Gunshot – groin
Smith, R.	Qtrmstr	*Harrier*	Mere Mere	13.08.63	Wounded Gunshot – scalp
Steer, J.	Ord	*Esk*	Tepapa	29.04.64	Wounded Bayonet – thigh
Stevenson, R.	Boy	*Curacoa*	Rangariri	20.11.63	Died/Wounds Gunshot – abdomen (died 21.11.63)
Tenam, T.	Ord	*Curacoa*	Tepapa	29.04.64	Wounded Gunshot – hip
Tidy, W.	AB	*Curacoa*	Rangariri	20.11.63	Killed Gunshot – head
Tozer, G.	Ord	*Niger*	Omata	28.03.60	Wounded Wound – thigh
Ward, R.	Gunr (RMA)	*Esk*	Tepapa	29.04.64	Wounded Gunshot – right thigh
Watkins, T.	Midn	*Curacoa*	Rangariri	20.11.63	Killed Gunshot – head
Watson, J.	Ord	*Curacoa*	Tepapa	29.04.64	Wounded Gunshot – left knee
Watts, M.	Gunr (RMA)	*Miranda*	Tepapa	29.04.64	Killed Tomahawk – head
Ween, C.	Gunr (RMA)	*Curacoa*	Tepapa	29.04.64	Wounded Gunshot – lower jaw
Woods, J.	Qtrmstr	*Curacoa*	Rangariri	20.11.63	Killed Gunshot – head
Young, G.	AB	*Harrier*	Tepapa	29.04.64	Wounded Gunshot – chest

H.M.S. *Calliope*

H.M.S. *Calliope* was a 6th Rate armed with 24 x 9 pdr and 4 x 3 pdr guns. Her tonnage was 717 bm and she was 130 x 35½ feet. She was built in Sheerness Dock Yard and launched on 5 October 1837. She was converted in 1860 into a floating chapel and five years later became a factory. The ship was finally broken up on 1 November 1883 at Devonport.

Notes on medal roll:

'AO 31 Jan 1870. Only those landed & actually engaged.'

New Zealand Medal for services in H.M.S. *Calliope* in 1846–47.

Adkins, J.	Fifer
Arthur, W.	Naval Cadet
Barrett, W.	Capt Missentop
Beard, W.	Caulker
Belsey, J.	AB
Beresford, H. B.	Lieutenant
Blake, J.	Capt Foretop
Blight, G.	Capt Forecastle
Brenchley, R.	Cox of Launch
Broadbelt, A.	Gunner's Mate
Canter, R.	Private
Carnegie, J.	Midshipman
Chant, S.	Private
Chappell, G.	Boy
Coombes, T.	AB
Creese, C.	Ord
Crozier, H. E.	Naval Cadet
Cullen, S.	Ord
Dennis, H.	Boatswain
Dickens, U.	Capt Maintop
Dodge, T.	Private
Dunsford, W.	Ord
Dyer, J.	Sergeant
Eastcott, G.	Capt Maintop
Easterbrook, C.	Private
Essary, R.	AB
Evans, J.	Private
Ferrero, J.	Capt Mizzentop
Friend, J.	Boy
Gibson, C.	Ord
Graham, R. B.	Master
Harrison, G. P.	Carpenter's Crew
Higginson, W.	AB
Horswill, J.	Private
Johns, W.	Private
Jones, T.	Capt Afterguard
Keightley, J.	AB
Lamer, A.	Boy
McKillop, H. F.	Midshipman
Martin, S.	AB

Maynard, H.	Boy
Mayne, J.	Private
Monks, H.	AB
Nicolas, B. G. W.	Midshipman
Payne, J.	AB
Phillips, J.	Ord
Polkinghorne, C. J.	2nd Master
Reeve, J.	Boy
Rook, A.	Ord
Ross, W.	Asst Surgeon
Scown, J.	Private
Smith, J.	Boatswain's Mate
Spratt, T.	Carpenter's Mate
Stanley, E.	Captain
Sullivan, C.	Carpenter's Crew
Susans, J.	Boy
Thorp, W.	Lieutenant
Tickle, J.	Sailmaker's Mate
Welsh, J.	Acting Gunner
West, H.	AB
Willcox, H.	Ord
Wright, J.	Captain's Cox

Noted on roll as Run:

Brown, J.	AB *Run 3.7.61.*

H.M.S. *Castor*

H.M.S. *Castor* was a 5th Rate armed with 36 x 32pdr guns. Her tonnage was 1,293 bm or 1,808 tons and she was 159 x 43 feet. She was built in Chatham Dock Yard and launched on 2 May 1832. She became a Royal Naval Reserve training ship in January 1860. She was sold on 25 August 1902 at Sheerness.

Notes on medal roll:

'AO 31 Jan 1870 No 449. Only those landed & actually engaged.'

New Zealand Medal for services in H.M.S. *Castor* in 1845-1846-1847.

Bailey, J.	AB
Baker, H.	AB
Bennett, W.	AB
Brown, A.	AB
Brown, W.	AB
Burdett, J.	AB
Burnham, J.	AB
Cator, R. P.	Midshipman
Charge, J.	Private
Chinnery, E.	Yeoman of Signals
Cock, M.	AB
Coe, J.	AB
Cornish, W. J.	Boy
Couch, E.	AB
Dingle, W.	AB
Ellery, G.	AB

Flaherty, J.	AB
Frazer, D.	AB
Goddard, H.	Private
Green, J. G.	Gun Room Steward
Haddon, J.	Private
Harris, J.	Private
Harrison, R. S.	Lieutenant (RM)
Hawke, R.	AB
Hedden, T.	AB
Henwright, T.	AB
Hoyle, C.	AB
Humphreys, H.	AB
Hutchings, J.	Ord
Hynes, M.	AB
Inkster, J.	AB
Irving, J.	Ord
James, J.	AB
Johnson, J.	AB
Johnson, N.	AB
Kemp, E. J.	Master's Asst
Kennedy, J. W. A.	Lieutenant
Kersey, G.	Capt Missentop
Kuhlman, J.	AB
Larkin, G.	Boy
Leveridge, F.	Ord
Martin, G.	Sick Berth Attn
McCann, T.	AB
McGill, T.	AB
McIllree, H.	AB
Merson, G. H.	Boy
Miller, J.	AB
Moor, W.	AB
Murphy, D.	AB
O'Malley, J.	AB
Otway, R. J.	Senior Lieutenant
Palmer, J.	AB
Pritchard, R. D.	Asst Surgeon
Reeby, J.	AB
Richardson, W.	AB
Sargent, W.	Capt of Hold
Shearer, R.	Sailmaker's Mate
Stephens, J.	AB
Taylor, W.	AB
Tippins, J. T.	AB
Walker, R.	Private
Warrell, A.	Private
Watkins, J.	Capt Maintop
Watts, S.	Corporal
Weymouth, J.	Capt Foretop
Wills, S.	AB
Wiltshire, W.	Gunner's Mate
Woods, T.	AB
Young, C.	Capt Missentop

H.M.S. *Driver*

H.M.S. *Driver* was a Wooden Paddle Sloop. Her tonnage was 1,058 bm and she was 180 x 36 feet.

She was built in Portsmouth Dock Yard and launched on 24 December 1840. She was wrecked in August 1861 on Mariguana Island.

Notes on medal roll:
'AO 31 Jan 1870 No 449. Only those landed & actually engaged.'

New Zealand Medal for services in H.M.S. *Driver* in 1845-1846-1847.

Alpe, A.	Master-at-Arms
Barnes, W.	Gunner
Bromley, C.	Lieutenant
Cobden, J.	Ord
Connolly, M.	Lieutenant
Darley, J. (or Darby)	AB
Harvey, J.	Quartermaster
Marcuard, C. R.	Lieutenant
Radmore, G. H.	Ord
Small, J.	Gunner (RMA)

H.E.I.C.S. *Elphinstone*

H.E.I.C.S. *Elphinstone* was a Sloop armed with 18 x 6 pdr guns. Her tonnage was 387 bm. She was built in Bombay Dock Yard and launched in 1824. She was sold in July 1862.

Notes on medal roll:
None.

New Zealand Medal for services in the H.E.I.C.S. *Elphinstone* in 1845-6-7

Broughton, F.	Asst Surgeon
Collins, R.	AB
Garrett, H. H.	Midshipman
Keys, J. A.	Paymaster
Simpson, J.	Gunner (Bombay Artillery)
Pengelley, W. H.	Midshipman

H.M.S. *Hazard*

H.M.S. *Hazard* was a Sloop armed with 18 x 6 pdr guns. Her tonnage was 431 bm and she was 110½ x 31 feet. She was built in Portsmouth Dock Yard and launched on 21 April 1837. She had been broken up by White of Cowes by 12 February 1866.

Notes on medal roll:
'Ships engaged with enemy 11 March 1845 – all on board entitled.'

New Zealand Medal for services in H.M.S. *Hazard* in 1845-6-7.

Adams, H.	Boatswain's Mate
Anderson, R.	AB
Baxter, J.	Capt Mizzentop
Calvin, M.	AB
Campbell, T.	AB
Channon, C.	AB
Chatfield, R.	Private
Clark, C.	Boatswain
Coles, G.	AB
Crawford, C.	AB
Edsell, H.	Private
Everett, J.	AB
Fisher, J.	Boy
Force, H.	Quartermaster
Glenister, J.	AB
Hughes, S.	Purser's Steward
Huthwaite, A. G. D.	Midshipman
Hyden, S.	AB
Kelly, H. J.	Clerk
Lacey, J.	AB
Morgan, E. E.	Lieutenant
Moubray, R. H.	Mate
Parr, G.	Private
Parrott, J. W.	Midshipman
Potter, J.	Private
Quin, J.	Boatswain's Mate
Reeves, R.	Capt Foretop
Robertson, D.	Commander
Robinson, J.	AB
Spain, D.	Midshipman
Tarplett, T.	AB
Thompson, J.	Carpenter's Mate
Tipper, W.	AB
Tripp, J.	Gunner's Mate
Veitch, J. T.	Acting Surgeon

H.M.S. *Inflexible*

H.M.S. *Inflexible* was a Wooden Paddle Sloop. Her tonnage was 1,122 bm and she was 190 x 36 feet. She was built in Pembroke Dock and launched on 12 April 1845. She was sold to Castle & Beech in 1864.

Notes on medal roll:
'AO 31 Jan No 449. Only those landed & actually engaged.'

New Zealand Medal for services in H.M.S. *Inflexible* in 1845-6-7.

Alford, J.	Private
Alldridge, J. C.	Paymaster
Austin, R.	Gunner (RMA)
Cole, S.	Ord
Cosby, H.	Gunner (RMA)
Cuming, W. H.	Naval Cadet
Eades, G.	Clerk's Assistant
Giddy, N.	Boy
Gordon, W. E. A.	Lieutenant
Harris, H.	Corporal (RMA)
Hayward, W.	Sergeant

Hird, W.	AB
Hornsby, R.	Private
Hoseason, J. C.	Commander
Johnson, F. M.	Boatswain's Mate
Lloyd, J.	Cooper's Crew
Roach, E.	AB
Stoddon, I.	AB
Turner, J.	Ropemaker
Weekes, G.	Stoker

H.M.S. *North Star*

H.M.S. *North Star* was a 6th Rate armed with 24 x 9 pdr and 4 x 3 pdr guns. Her tonnage was 501 bm and she was 114 x 32 feet. She was built at Woolwich Dock Yard and launched on 7 December 1824. She had been broken up at Chatham by 15 March 1860.

Notes on medal roll:
'AO 31 Jan No 449. Only those landed & actually engaged.'

New Zealand Medal for services in H.M.S. *North Star* in 1845-6-7.

Adshead, J.	Capt Missentop
Amey, J.	AB
Andrews, R.	Sergeant
Blatchley, J.	AB
Burton, J.	Ord
Capon, H.	Capt Foretop
Chubb, G.	AB
Curtis, A. J.	Lieutenant
Draper, E.	Private
Forbes, C. S.	Midshipman
Gilpin, J. D.	Clerk
Hagar, W.	Private
Hooper, R.	Capt Foretop
Howick, H.	AB
Jackson, G.	AB
Jago, W.	Sailmaker's Mate
Jasper, T.	Boatswain
Jerrome, J. (or *Jerram*)	Ord
Johnson, G.	Lieutenant
Kelly, J.	Captain's Cox
Langford, W. B.	Captain (RM)
McDonald, J.	Capt Forecastle
Maslin, J.	Private
Mould, G. H.	Boy
Noice, R. J.	Ord
Oliver, C. F.	AB
Parsons, T.	AB
Partridge, J.	Drummer
Patter, J.	Private
Pope, C.	Ord
Saunders, W. McK.	Acting Surgeon
Scott, E.	AB

Smith, T.	Capt Missentop
Spearing, E.	Ord
Trezise, T.	Gunner's Mate
Vizard, T.	Private
Waight, J.	AB
Webb, G.	Quartermaster
Willcocks, W.	Capt Afterguard
Woodman, G.	Boatswain's Mate
Woodman, T.	Boatswain's Mate

H.M.S. *Osprey*

H.M.S. *Osprey* was a Brig armed with 10 x 32 pdr and 2 x 18 pdr guns. Her tonnage was 425 bm and she was 101½ x 32 feet. She was built in Portsmouth Dock Yard and launched on 2 April 1844. She was wrecked on 11 March 1846 off Hokianga, New Zealand.

Notes on medal roll:
'AO 31 Jan 1870, No 449. Only those landed & actually engaged.'

New Zealand Medal for services in H.M.S. *Osprey* in 1845-6-7

Brown, W.	Private
Cruys, W. H.	AB
Division, N.	AB
Grimes, T.	Capt Maintop
Hampshire, J.	Private
Lewis, F.	AB
Parish, R.	Capt Foretop
Pearce, J.	Boy
Taylor, J.	Private
Traveller, W.	Painter
White, J.	Colour Sergeant

H.M.S. *Racehorse*

H.M.S. *Racehorse* was a Sloop armed with 18 x 9 pdr guns. Her tonnage was 438 bm and she was 110 x 31 feet. She was built in Plymouth Dock Yard and launched on 24 May 1830. She became a coal hulk in 1860 and was finally sold in 1901.

Notes on medal roll:
'AO 31 Jan 1870 No 449. Only those landed & actually engaged.'

New Zealand Medal for services in H.M.S. *Racehorse* in 1845-6-7

Ayres, R. B.	Ord
Black, J.	Capt Maintop
Bland, A.	Lieutenant
Blyth, H.	Capt Maintop
Brown, J.	Boy
Brown, T.	Quartermaster
Bubb, J.	Private

Butler, J.	Private
Clarke, J.	Gunner's Mate
Collins, P.	Cooper
Crew, J.	Commander's Cook
Dunning J. S.	AB
Edwards, J.	Fifer
Flynn, W.	Ord
Fry, J.	Colour Sergeant
Handford, R.	Capt Forecastle
Hext, J.	Ord
Hooper, R.	Gunner
Hoyle, T.	AB
Lawrence, I.	Corporal
Lee, C.	Capt Afterguard
McLoghlin, J.	Boy
Parkman, J. R.	Capt Foretop
Parnell, W.	Private
Pascoe, W.	Capt Maintop
Richards, J.	AB
Ross, C.	Ord
Sammells, H.	Ord
Scott, C.	Naval Cadet
Shea, J.	Ord
Skedgell, H.	Private
Tippett, R. R.	Ord
Tucker, W. R.	Sailmaker
Whitburn, W.	Carpenter's Mate
Widger, J.	Private
Yarnold, C.	Private

H.M.S. Brisk

H.M.S. Brisk was a Wooden Screw Sloop armed with 2 x 68 pdr and 12 x 32 pdr guns. Her tonnage was 1,087 bm and she was 190½ x 35 feet. She was built in Woolwich Dock Yard and launched on 2 June 1851. She was sold on 31 January 1870 into Mercantile service.

Notes on medal roll:

'AO 24 Jan 1870 No 355 aquaints that officer and men of the *Brisk* were never engaged under fire, they cannot be allowed the medal. 13 officers & men only, subsequently granted the medal.'

New Zealand Medal for services in H.M.S. *Brisk* in 1865

Bell, J. J. F.	Sub-Lieutenant
Churchill, J.	AB
Collings, G.	Cox Pinnace
Crow, B.	Ldg Seaman
Fitton, C. S.	Lieutenant
Harvey, E. J.	Ord
Hunt, T.	Ldg Seaman
Long, J.	Capt Maintop
Lyons, P.	Ord
Pomeroy, E.	AB
Pook, J.	AB

Stevens, S.	Ldg Seaman
Stoale, G. H.	Master's Assistant

H.M.S. Cordelia

H.M.S. *Cordelia* was a Wooden Screw Sloop armed with 11 x 32 pdr guns. Her tonnage was 579 bm and she was 151 x 29 feet. She was built in Pembroke Dock and launched on 3 July 1856. She was sold on 12 May 1870 to Marshall at Plymouth.

Notes on medal roll:

'Naval Brigade only.'

New Zealand Medal for services in H.M.S. *Cordelia* in 1860-61.

Angeley, R.	Gunner
Ashweek, E.	Private
Berry, J.	Capt Forecastle
Billings, J.	Corporal (RMA)
Brice, R.	AB
Burke, S. J.	Asst Surgeon
Barron, R.	Capt Afterguard
Chapman, J. W.	Ldg Seaman
Ferris, T.	Capt Maintop
Fosberry, C.	Gunner (RMA)
Hamlyn, G.	Private
Harvey, R.	Capt Maintop
Hooper, S.	Capt Foretop
Jackson, D.	Capt Missentop
Lambell, W.	AB
Leach, R. C.	Lieutenant
Lewis, J.	Private
Lowry, J.	AB
May, J.	Gunner's Mate
Medlow, W.	Private
Melluish, W.	Private
Rogers, M.	Ord
Russle, J.	Private
Ryder, E.	Carpenter's Crew
Self, H.	Captain's Cox
Squires, E.	AB
Vaughan, J.	AB
Vernon, C. E. H.	Commander
Warner, T.	Private

H.M.S. Curacoa

H.M.S. *Curacoa* was a Wooden Screw Frigate armed with 1 x 10 in and 30 x 32 pdr guns. Her tonnage was 1,570 bm and she was 192 x 43 feet. She was built in Pembroke Dock and launched on 13 April 1854. She had been broken up by 17 July 1869.

Notes on medal roll:

'Naval Brigade & Flotilla Only.'

New Zealand Medal for services in
H.M.S. *Curacoa* in 1863–66.

Adamson, J.	Ord
Alexander, H. McC.	**Lieutenant**
*Allene, W. J.	Ord
Andrews, G.	Boy
Appleton, J.	Ord
Atkins, M.	Sergeant (RMA)
Atteridge, T.	AB
Baker, W.	Gunner (RMA)
Barry, P.	Stoker
Bates, J.	Gunner (RMA)
Batney, J.	AB
Baulch, J.	Cooper
Beacham, J.	Carpenter's Mate
Bedford, A.	Private
Bedow, C.	Ldg Seaman

Roll states, 'Waikato Flt. 21 Oct 63–31 Jan 64.'

Biggs, W.	Private
Botterill, E. H.	Boy
Boulton, J. G.	Master's Assistant
Bowman, C. P.	Captain's Cox
Bradshaw, W.	Ord
Burnie, W.	Gunner (RMA)
Burns, T. H.	Ord
Burrows, G.	Ldg Seaman
Carney, J.	Private
Carroll, J.	Ord
Chattell, F.	Ord
Clark, W.	AB
Coak, H. J.	AB
Cockcraft, W. La T.	Lieutenant (RMA)
Cockle, J.	AB
Collis, J.	Boy
Cook, J.	W. Officer's Cook
Cooke, B.	Cox Cutter
Cookman, F.	Drummer
Corvell, F.	Private
Cox, H.	Sergeant
Cranbrook, G.	Ord
*Dobbs, G.	Boy
Dollar, T.	**AB**
Doran, D.	Stoker
Doughty, W. G.	Master-at-Arms
Downer, G.	Boy
Elvin, J.	Private
(or Elven)	
Eves, J. S.	AB
Fane, R.	Cox Pinnace
Filbin, P.	Private
Flood, W.	Asst Paymaster
Foley, W.	Private
Foljambe, C. G. S.	Midshipman
Forrell, W.	Bandsman
Fox, W.	**AB**
French, H.	AB
Gardiner, W.	Gunner (RMA)

Garratt, E.	Corporal
Gillingham, J.	Gunner (RMA)
*Godwin, E.	AB
Goldsmith, H.	Gunner (RMA)
Goodenough, G.	Private
Goodwin, J.	Gunner (RMA)
Graham, H. J.	AB
Graham, J.	Ord
Gray, A.	Asst Engineer
Gray, A.	Ldg Seaman
Green, E.	Private
Green W.	Ord
Grieve, S.	Gunner (RMA)
Gumbrell, H.	Ord
Haley, T.	AB
Harris, H.	Boy
Harris, T.	Private
Harrison, J. G. W.	Midshipman
Hart, G.	Boy
Hayles, S.	**Ord**
Hayter, G. T.	Capt Mast
Heathcote, W. E.	Midshipman
Hendey, C.	Ord
Henly, T. D.	Ldg Seaman
Hibberd, W.	Captain's Steward
Higginson, G. M. J.	Asst Paymaster
Hill, S.	AB
Hinks, H.	Stoker
Holden, S.	Boy
Hudin, F.	Boy
Hudson, F. E.	Midshipman
Hunt, C. G.	Midshipman
Hunt, G. L.	Boy
Jackson, T. E.	Bombardier
James, D.	Private
James, J.	Gunner's Mate
James, T.	AB
James, T. W.	Capt Forecastle
Jenkins, C.	Armourer's Crew
Jerram, T.	Ord
John, E.	Boy
Johns, B.	Stoker
Jones, J.	Quartermaster
Kendall, J. D.	Ord
Kerrison, C.	Shipwright
Kilgour, W.	Ldg Seaman
Kill, C.	AB
King, J.	AB
Kissick, A.	Ord
Kitchener, H.	Ord
Klintberg, A. F.	Lieutenant
Liddell, G.	Clerk
Loxley, G.	Ord
McDonald, A.	AB
McGregor, R.	Ord
MacKenzie, J.	Boatswain's Mate
Mackley, J. H.	Ldg Seaman

Mansell, J.	Private
Mansell, T.	SB Attendant
Manuel, A.	Boy
Marriott, H.	Capt Foretop
Marsnew, R.	Boatswain's Mate
Martin, T.	Capt Forecastle
Mawbey, E.	Ship's Corporal
Messer, A. B.	Asst Surgeon
Millman, E. W. M.	Paymaster
Milward, W.	Gunner (RMA)
Mindry, R.	Gunner
Morgan, D.	Boy
Morris, G. de C.	Clerk
Moss, W.	Gunner (RMA)
*Murphy, M.	AB
Murray, W. F.	Midshipman
Naggs, J.	Quartermaster
Nightingale, W.	Gunner's Mate
Pafford, G.	Ord
Page, G.	Stoker
Parnell, G.	AB
Parker, P. R. H.	Lieutenant
Payne, Rev. S. W.	Chaplain & N Instr
Phillimore, H. B.	Commander
Picken, R.	Surgeon
Pickles, T. F.	Boy
Pilbeam, A.	Ord
Pitt, H.	Boatswain's Mate
Pool, W.	Ship's Corporal
Prestley, H.	Private
Price, J. W.	AB
*Prince, H.	Capt Cook's Asst
Rabbitt, W.	Ord
Reed, J.	Ldg Seaman
Reynolds, W.	Ord
Richards, J.	Private
Ricketts, H.	Private
Robinson, T.	Private
Rowe, J. F.	AB
Rudkins, J. T.	Capt Missentop
Sandford, G.	Gunner (RMA)
Scott, I. D.	Ord
Seymour, A.	AB
Shillady, A.	Ord
Simpson, W.	Ord
Snewin, F.	AB
Sparkes, E. B.	Boy
Sparks, W. H.	AB
Springel, A.	Capt Missentop
also entered on roll as Springle	
Stacey, W.	Boy
Stent, E.	Ord
Stevens, C.	Ord
Stewart, G. H.	Domestic
Sutton, T.	AB
Taylor, T.	Private
Terry, R.	Ord
Terry, W.	Ldg Seaman
Tester, J.	AB
Thomas, E.	AB
Timbrell, G.	Ord
Toby, W.	AB
Tompkins, F.	Private
Treffry, H.	Midshipman
Turtle, G. E.	Ord & Carpenter's Crew
Wade, J.	Gunner (RMA)
Walsh, E.	Ord
Watson, J.	**Ord**
Ween, C.	**Gunner (RMA)**
Whelan, T.	Private
Whitcombe, W.	Capt Afterguard
White, H.	Private
White, T.	Ldg Seaman
Wilden, W.	Private
Wiseman, Sir W. S.	Commodore
Witty, G. R.	Ord
Wyatt, H. W.	Secretary
Young, H.	AB

Noted on roll as Run:

Jolin, E.	Boy *Run Oct 1871*

H.M.S. *Eclipse*

H.M.S. *Eclipse* was a Wooden Screw Sloop armed with 2 x 68 pdr and 2 x 32 pdr guns. Her tonnage was 700 bm and she was 185 x 28½ feet. She was built at Millwall by Scott Russell and launched on 18 September 1860. She was broken up at Sheerness in July 1867.

Notes on medal roll:

'Men with flotilla. The ship also shelled the enemy's positions on 4 June 1863 & 21 September 1865 & AO 3 June 1870. 1852 granted the medal to all actually engaged under fire. List supplied by captain.'

New Zealand Medal for services in H.M.S. *Eclipse* in 1863–66.

Allen, J.	AB
Archer, T.	Private
Bailey, F.	Boy
Baker, J.	Ord
Balcom, H.	Boy
Bath, T.	Ord
Belson, B. G. A.	Lieutenant
Birkenshaw, W.	Private
Bishop, H.	Ord
Bodsworth, J.	Private
Boughey, W. F.	Lieutenant
Browning, F.	Boy
Byrne, J.	Gunner's Mate
Callaghan, E.	Boy
Callaway, F. E.	AB

Clay, W.	Capt Foretop
Cleave, R.	AB
Cooper, W.	Stoker
Corker, G.	**Acting Corporal**
Corr, J.	Private
Corrie, A. Le B.	Asst Paymaster
Course, R.	Gunner (RMA)
Cowling, R.	Private
Davis, J.	Boy
Dawkins, J.	Stoker
Day, J.	Private
Dempster, E.	Stoker
Donald, W. R.	Engineer
Donnelly, W.	Stoker
Dow, R.	Boy
Emery, W.	Ord
Fremantle, E. R.	Commander
Gilbert, W.	Asst Engineer
Green, W. H.	Carpenter's Crew
Hawkins, J.	Boatswain
Hendey, R.	Captain's Steward
Higgins, J.	Stoker
Hutchison, W. B.	Paymaster
Kemp, G.	Boy
Kettle, J.	2/Capt Foretop
McDowell, W.	Ord
McFarlane, J.	Asst Engineer
Maitland, D.	Gunner (RMA)
Mason, W.	Ldg Seaman
Mayne, R. C.	**Commander**
Metters, H. J.	Gunner's Mate
Minkey, F.	AB
Moody, E.	Ldg Stoker
Newton, W.	Caulker's Mate
Nicholls, L.	Ldg Stoker
Norris, T.	Quartermaster
Padbury, J.	Gunner (RMA)
Parker, E. J.	Gunner
Perry, J.	Stoker
Phillips, B.	Stoker
Pollington, E.	Boatswain's Mate
Randall, R.	Quartermaster
Rennie, W.	Carpenter's Crew
Richards, R.	Stoker
Rintoul, J.	Blacksmith
Rouse, J.	Chief Carpenter's Mate
Rowe, H.	Private
Scholefield, C. J.	Sub-Lieutenant
Sims, J.	AB

Roll states, 'Duplicate refused as original medal was pledged.'

Southam, H.	Ldg Seaman
Stuckey, G.	Ord
Swain, M.	Boy
Taylor, G.	Private
Taylor, R.	Captain's Cox
Tucker, G.	Stoker

Underdown, W. G.	Ship's Cook
Wain, T.	Corporal (RMA)
Walwin, E.	Ord
Weeks, J.	Boy
Willis, S. A.	Surgeon

H.M.S. *Esk*

H.M.S. *Esk* was a Wooden Screw Corvette armed with 20 x 8 in and 1 x 68 pdr guns. Her tonnage was 1,169 bm and she was 192 x 38½ feet. She was built at Millwall by Scott Russell and launched on 12 June 1854. She was broken up at Portsmouth in 1870.

Notes on medal roll:
'Naval Brigade & Flotilla Only.'

New Zealand Medal for services in H.M.S. *Esk* in 1863–66.

Anderson, W.	Capt Afterguard
Ashley, A.	Gunner (RMA)
Bacon, G. W.	Ord
Barber, W.	Boy
Barlow, J.	Cox Launch
*Barnes, E.	AB
Beckett, J.	Quartermaster
Bell, C. E.	Midshipman
Bennett, J.	Gunner (RMA)
Black, G.	Ord
Boden, F.	AB
Bowden, A.	**AB**
Bowling, J.	Private

Medal roll shows two entries for this man indicating that two medals were issued.

Brading, G.	Ldg Seaman
Bridger, W.	Capt Maintop
Brown, D.	AB
Bruce, J.	Capt Missentop
Bull, H.	Gunner (RMA)
Burge, W. H.	AB
Burkenshaw, W. A.	AB
Chapman, W. H.	AB
Childs, W.	Boy
*Chowne, J. H. F.	Midshipman
Clark, B. F.	Senior Lieutenant
Cooper, I.	Ldg Seaman
Cribb, J.	Ord
D'Arcy, J.	Boy
Davis, J.	Gunner (RMA)
Donley, J.	AB
Donowa, V. C.	Capt Maintop
Downman, H. G.	Clerk
Dredge, J.	AB
Duff, G. G.	**Lieutenant**
Evans, J.	Caulker
Farley, E.	AB
Farrell, J.	Gunner's Mate

Flannery, J.	Private	Swayne, J. C.	Boy
Gardner, R. B.	Lieutenant (RMA)	Tatton, W. H.	Gunner
Gill, R.	Carpenter	Taylor, J.	Boatswain's Mate
Goldsmith, T.	Boy	Templeton, J. H.	AB
Grant, W.	Boy	Terry, E.	Carpenter's Crew
Grissell, C. E.	Midshipman	Thompson, J.	AB
Grunsell, G.	Boy	Tomlinson, R.	Private
Hale, T.	Gunner (RMA)	Tompson, J.	Private
Hanson, W.	Boy	Toy, R.	AB
Harris, T.	AB	Trent, T.	Ord
Harrison, C.	Boy	Trigger, R.	Drummer
Hazzard, E.	Ord	Viney, E.	Gunner (RMA)
Humphrey, J.	Boy	Wadge, F.	Boy
Hunt, C.	Captain's Cox	Walder, T. J.	AB
Jeffery, R.	**AB**	**Ward, R.**	**Gunner (RMA)**
Keachie, W.	Capt Missentop	Wearne, W.	Capt Missentop
Kelly, T.	AB	Webb, W.	Ord
Kent, G.	Ord	Welsh, J.	Capt Afterguard
Knight, J.	**Capt Forecastle**	White, J.	Carpenter's Mate
Lindsay, C.	Midshipman	Whitehead, J.	Boy
Lindsey, W.	Ord	Williams, J.	Capt Foretop
McLeod, N.	Stoker	Wiseman, W.	Midshipman
Malham, E.	AB	Wood, C. E.	Midshipman
Manning, F. N.	Asst Surgeon	Wyard, G.	Gunner (RMA)
Marson, W.	Private	Young, G.	Sergeant (RMA)
Martin, E.	**AB**		

Noted on roll as Run:

Sargeant, J.	AB	*Run 11 Oct 1865*
White, J.	Capt Missentop	*Run 6 June 1864*

Martin, G.	Boatswain's Mate
Martin, J.	Boy
Masters, R.	Gunner (RMA)
Maynard, W.	AB
Moquet, P.	Ldg Seaman
Morgan, J. D.	Ord
Mortimer, H.	Carpenter's Crew
Mortimer, T. H.	Armourer
Moseley, R.	Gunner (RMA)
Murphy, M.	Private
Musgrave, A. J. W.	Lieutenant
Newman, T.	AB
Oclee, G. R.	AB
O'Connor, M.	Gunner (RMA)
Oldham, E. H.	Midshipman
Orlebar, V. B.	Lieutenant
Perrin, A.	Ord
Quick, S.	Gunner (RMA)
Randall, G.	Ord
Ratty, C.	Stoker
Rawlings, J.	Private
*Read, S.	Boy
Richardson, G.	Boy
Robins, F. T.	Paymaster
Rounds, G.	AB
Rowe, R.	AB
Sherwood, E.	Gunner (RMA)
Silver, E.	Gunner (RMA)
Simmonds, F.	Ord
Skinner, T.	Boy
Smith, W.	Ord
Springgay, J.	Boy

H.M.S. *Falcon*

H.M.S. *Falcon* was a Wooden Screw Sloop armed with 17 x 32 pdr guns. Her tonnage was 748 bm and she was 160 x 31½ feet. She was built in Pembroke Dock and launched on 10 August 1854. She was sold on 27 September 1869 to Marshall at Plymouth.

Notes on medal roll:

'Those checked for service on shore and in Flotilla under fire. Vessel shelled enemy's positions on 29 April 1864, but medal was not allowed for this service.'

New Zealand Medal for services in H/M.S. *Falcon* in 1863–66.

Donegan, B.	Gunner (RMA)
Hammond, G.	Private
Hance, A.	Drummer
Hitchcock, J.	Private
Inskip, W.	Private
Jopson, E.	Private
Kingsell, W.	Private
Lewis, W.	Gunner (RMA)
Lucas, J.	Private
Morgan, W.	Private

Needham, G.   Private
Waugh, I.   Asst Surgeon

H.M.S. *Harrier*

H.M.S. *Harrier* was a Wooden Screw Sloop armed with 17 x 32pdr guns. Her tonnage was 747 bm and she was 160 x 32 feet. She was built in Pembroke Dock and launched on 13 May 1854. Her breaking up was completed in December 1866 at Portsmouth.

Notes on medal roll:

'Naval Brigade & Flotilla Only.'

New Zealand Medal for services in H.M.S. *Harrier* in 1863–66.

Allen, J. P.	Chief Engineer
Allen, R.	Ord
Barton, S.	Sick Berth Attn
Bellen, A.	AB
Bennett, E.	Private
Bennett, J.	Gunner (RMA)
Benney, J.	Drummer
Bolton, T. H.	Ord
Borrett, C.	Ord
Brazier, D.	AB
Brister, G.	Ord
Bristow, G.	Cooper
Brown, J. J.	AB
Colenut, J.	AB
Cox, W. R.	AB
Dalley, E.	Carpenter
Darling, D.	Ord
Duff, C. W.	Ord
Easther, F. J.	Lieutenant
Falcon, T. H.	Lieutenant
Foster, T.	Colour Sergeant
Gale, E. H.	Boy
Hilston, D.	Asst Surgeon
Hoddstock, W.	Private
Hodge, T.	Private
Hopkins, P.	Private
Houseman, J.	Corporal (RMA)
Hunt, R. S.	Lieutenant
Ibbotson, S.	Private
Johnson, G.	AB
Johnson, J. W.	Ord
Jones, J.	Ord
Jones, J. A.	Master's Assistant
Kennedy, J.	AB
Knight, G.	Gunner's Mate
Lansdown, G.	Stoker
Littlejohn, B. J.	Quartermaster
Lockhart, J.	Quartermaster
Lockie, A.	**AB**
Love, W.	Carpenter's Crew
McPhail, D.	Stoker
Marchant, C.	Ldg Stoker

Marshall, J.	AB
Maunder, H. A.	Ord
May, H.	Ord
Mitchell, S.	Capt Foretop

Roll states, *'Awarded V.C. Applied for dup, but original found and returned to daughter.'*

Moore, J. E.	Signalman
Muir, G. G.	AB
Nancarrow, T. H.	Ord
Nelson, C.	Sailmaker's Mate
Nicholson, J.	Carpenter's Mate
Pallatt, J.	**Ldg Seaman**
Pettman, A.	Ord
Pocock, W.	AB
Randell, C.	Ord
Revill, A. J.	Ord
Roberts, G.	Ord
Rodda, T.	AB
Rose, H.	Blacksmith
Russell, J.	Stoker
Russell, T.	Ldg Seaman
Scrivener, H. A.	Asst Paymaster
Smith, G.	Boy
Smith, P.	Gunner
Smith, R.	Boatswain's Mate
Snudden, T.	AB
Stares, W.	2/Capt Maintop
Strickland, G.	Capt Forecastle
Strugnell, G.	Capt Forecastle
Sullivan, F. W.	Commander
Thacker, S.	Corporal (RMA)
Thomas, C.	Ord
Tringham, P. R.	Gun Room Steward
Walker, H. J.	2/Capt Foretop
Walker, W.	Boy
Warn, W.	Shipwright
Wells, N.	AB
Whitehead, W.	Ord
Williamson, G.	Boy
Young, G.	**AB**

H.M.S. *Himalaya*

H.M.S. *Himalaya* was an Iron Screw Troopship. Her tonnage was 3,553 bm or 4,690 tons and she was 340 x 46 feet. She was built by Mare of Blackwall and launched on 24 May 1853. She was purchased in July 1854. In December 1895 she became a coal hulk and was renamed C.60. She was sold on 28 September 1920 to E. W. Payne and was sunk in 1940 during an air attack on Portland.

Notes on medal roll:

'Captain Lacey only entitled.'

New Zealand Medal for services in H.M.S. *Himalaya* in 1863–66.

Lacey, E.	Captain

H.M.S. *Iris*

H.M.S. *Iris* was a 6th Rate armed with 24 x 9 pdr and 4 x 3 pdr guns. Her tonnage was 906 bm and she was 131 x 40½ feet. She was built in Pembroke Dock and launched on 14 July 1840. She was sold on 16 October 1869 as a cable vessel.

Notes on medal roll:
'Naval Brigade Only.'

New Zealand Medal for services in H.M.S. *Iris* in 1860-61.

Alderton, R.	AB
Atkins, J.	Ord
Baker, H.	AB
Bent, T.	Lieutenant (RMA)
Brown, J.	AB
Buckle, W. V. J.	Gunner
Burtenshaw, W.	Capt Maintop
Burton, G.	AB
Catmore, D.	AB
Cave, H.	Capt Foretop
Chiverton, W.	AB
Coleman, W.	Private
Connolly, W.	Asst Surgeon
Connor, M.	AB
Cooke, C. M.	AB
Cooper, J. G.	AB
Cooper, W.	Capt Forecastle
Crisp, J.	AB
Crohan, H. F.	Midshipman
Deeks, J.	Sergeant
Fagg, W.	Ldg Seaman
Fox, J.	Capt Foretop
Frogley, J.	Boatswain
Frost, W.	Sailmaker
Gambier, J. W.	Midshipman
Gibson, W.	Quartermaster
Golding, C.	Shipwright
Gooch, W.	Private
Gray, F.	AB
*Gray, G.	Boy
Harris, T.	AB
Harris, W.	Capt Afterguard
Heath, W.	Capt Mast
Heneage, G. R.	Midshipman
Henley, W.	Boatswain's Mate
Hickmott, W. R.	Private
Hodgman, J.	Capt Missentop
Hume, F. A.	Lieutenant
Jarrold, J.	Boatswain's Mate
Johnston, F. A.	2nd Master
Jones, J.	AB
Langdon, H.	AB
Loring, W.	Commodore
Luckett, T.	AB
Medley, S. M.	Lieutenant
Mitchell, W. R.	AB
Morfee, G. W.	Ldg Seaman
Mower, R.	Private
Murphy, J.	AB
Newing, S.	Capt Maintop
Newman, G.	Ldg Seaman
Nicholls, R.	Private
North, C.	Capt Foretop
Peerless, J.	AB
Perry, S.	Private
Pierce, R. H.	Musician
Press, H.	Ord
Reynolds, G.	Private
Rogers, R.	Private
Sayer, C.	Private
Scane, J.	Private
*Singleton, W. H.	AB
Snook, W.	Captain's Cox
Spence, C. H.	Yeoman of Signals
Stanford, C.	AB
Ward, P.	AB
Whiley, W.	Carpenter's Mate
Whiteway, G.	Private
Whittaker, J. H.	AB
Wild, T.	AB
Wilson, G.	AB
Wright, H.	Gunner's Mate

H.M.S. *Miranda*

H.M.S. *Miranda* was a Wooden Screw Sloop armed with 2 x 7 in and 4 x 64 pdr guns. Her tonnage was 1,039 bm and she was 185 x 34½ feet. She was built in Sheerness Dock Yard and launched on 18 March 1851. She was sold to C. Lewis on 2 December 1869.

Notes on medal roll:
'Flotilla Only.'

New Zealand Medal for services in H.M.S. *Miranda* in 1863-66.

Adams, G.	Private
Alton, G.	**Gunner (RMA)**
Andrew, J. F.	Quartermaster
Andrews, W.	Ord
Austin, D.	Corporal
Barnes, G.	Paymaster
Barnes, H. J.	Capt Afterguard
Barrett, J.	Capt Forecastle
Barrett, J.	AB
Benttell, H.	Ord
Bettle, W.	Private
Bishop, T.	Gunner (RMA)
Bone, W.	Stoker
Boon, F. W.	AB
Broadley, G.	Quartermaster
Browning, W.	Blacksmith

Buntin, J.	Private
Bryan, M.	**AB**
Chalkley, W.	Captain's Cox
Chiswell, J.	Ldg Seaman
Chote, A.	Stoker
Claringbold, G.	**Ldg Seaman**
Clark, H.	Carpenter's Mate
Clews, W.	Stoker
Cockell, J.	AB
Collins, J.	AB
Cooper, W.	Stoker
Cope, T. E. B.	Master's Assistant
Corbet, F. C.	Master
Cox, W.	Ord
Cracknell, T. R.	Ord
Craig, A.	AB
Crocombe, J.	AB
Davitt, T.	Private
Downes, E. D. P.	**Lieutenant**
Duncan, J.	Ord
English, J.	**Capt Maintop**
Fox, M.	Capt Afterguard
Galling, T.	**Ldg Seaman**
Glassington, H.	Boatswain's Mate
Greenham, W.	AB
Griggs, E.	Ord
Hammick, R. F.	**Lieutenant**
Handley, J.	Private
Harding, R.	Asst Surgeon
Harland, W.	AB
Hollywood, I.	Carpenter's Mate
Hurlestone, G.	Ord
Jago, E. W.	Asst Paymaster
Jenkins, R.	Captain
Jordan, R.	Signalman
Lambert, W.	Private
McCollan, J.	Private
McDonald, D.	AB
*Martin, T.	AB
Metters, E. E.	Ldg Seaman
Miller, W. A.	Fifer & Bugler
Moody, P. T.	Private
Morrison, J.	Private
Murray, G.	Sergeant
Noakes, J.	**Boatswain's Mate**
Nolan, J.	Ord
Nunn, T. S.	Engineer
Purvis, F. J.	AB
Quick, R.	Private
Quinton, J.	Capt Foretop
Randle, T.	Ldg Seaman
Rastrick, J. L.	Asst Engineer
Reeves, R.	Capt Maintop
Ruthven, S.	**AB**
Sheepwash, G.	Ord
Slade, H.	Surgeon
Smith, H.	AB

Smith, W.	AB
Spain, T.	AB
Spencer, H.	AB
Still, H.	Corporal (RMA)
Synnett, J.	Boy
Taylor, J.	Stoker
Terale, C.	Colour Sergeant
Thompson, J.	AB
Varney, G.	Ord
Vercoe, S.	Ldg Seaman
Vince, C. F.	AB
Ward, G. T.	Gunner's Mate
White, H.	AB
White, W.	Sailmaker
Wilson, C.	Private
Woods, J. H.	Boy
Yeo, J.	AB
Young, R.	Ord

H.M.S. *Niger*

H.M.S. *Niger* was a Wooden Screw Sloop armed with 2 x 68 pdr and 12 x 32 pdr guns. Her tonnage was 1,013 bm and she was 190 x 35 feet. She was built in Woolwich Dock Yard and launched on 18 November 1846. She was sold on 2 December 1869 to Castle.

Notes on medal roll:
'Naval Brigade only. Not granted for service in ship when she fired on Wariea Pah.'

New Zealand Medal for services in H.M.S. *Niger* in 1860–61.

Atkins, W.	Quartermaster
Ball, W.	Ord
Bardens, H.	AB
Barlow, C.	Capt of Mast
Beech, S.	Gunner (RMA)
Bennett, J.	Ord
Blake, W. H.	**Lieutenant**
Blunden, J.	AB
Brian, P.	Ldg Seaman
Bristo, C.	AB
Bunyan, J.	AB
Clark, W.	**Private**
Collins, C.	Ord
Connor, J. T.	Capt Missentop
Craxford, A.	Gunner (RMA)
Ewell, E.	AB
Gassiot, S.	Midshipman
Goulthorpe, W.	AB
Grant, F.	Drummer
Griffin, J.	Capt Afterguard
Hubert, J.	AB
Hyde, W. H.	Asst Paymaster
Jones, J.	AB

Jones, J.	Sergeant (RMA)
Karslake, W. C.	Midshipman
Lambert, H. W.	Ship's Steward Assistant
Laurenson, R. C. P.	Asst Surgeon
Ledger, E. T.	Capt Foretop
Ledger, R. W.	Ldg Seaman
Lee, J. T.	Ldg Seaman
McDonald, W.	Stoker
Medcalf, W.	Sergeant
Morey, J.	Gunner (RMA)
Myers, J.	Private
Netherclift, W. H.	AB
New, W.	AB
Odgers, W.	Ldg Seaman
Oliver, S.	AB
Palmer, W.	**Private**
Parr, G.	Cox of Launch
Patrick, W.	Surgeon
Pizzey, T.	Blacksmith
Potter, N. J.	Gunner

*Roll states, 'Discharged Service by Court
Martial 8 July 1864.'*

Powell, D. W.	Boatswain's Mate
Price, T. C.	Midshipman
Pugh, T.	Private
Pryer, T.	Capt of Mast
Richardson, J. M.	AB
Rowbotham, G.	Gunner (RMA)
Searle, H.	Sailmaker's Mate
Skeggs, H. J.	Ord
Smyth, W. W.	Acting Mate
Snead, W. J.	AB
Sollors, J.	Gunner (RMA)
Taylor, J.	Private
Theobald, C. B.	Midshipman
Thorne, H.	Gunner (RMA)
Till, W.	Gunner (RMA)
Villiers, A. J.	Lieutenant
Walker, J.	AB
Ward, E.	Capt Maintop
Webb, H.	Ord
Wells, J. C.	Lieutenant
White, H. W.	Asst Engineer
Williams, J.	Private
Wilson, J.	Gunner's Mate

H.M.S. *Pelorus*

H.M.S. *Pelorus* was a Wooden Corvette armed with 20 x 8 in and 1 x 66 pdr guns. Her tonnage was 1,462 bm and she was 200 x 40 feet. She was built in Devonport Dock Yard and launched on 5 February 1857. She was broken up in 1869.

Notes on medal roll:

'Naval Brigade Only.'

New Zealand Medal for services in H.M.S. *Pelorus* in 1860–61.

Adams, G.	Private
Anderson, J.	Midshipman
Andrews, W.	Ord
Anthony, J.	Quartermaster
Avent, T.	Cox of Launch
Baker, J.	Private
Baker, W.	Private
Barham, H.	Gunner (RMA)
Bassett, A.	AB
Batt, J.	Ldg Seaman
Battiscombe, A. H. W.	Lieutenant
Beer, T.	Ord
Belford, J.	AB
Blake, T.	AB
Board, A. J.	Ship's Steward Assistant
Board, W.	AB
Body, F.	Ord
Bond, J.	Ord
Bowden, A.	AB
Branston, H.	Gunner (RMA)
Bryant, J.	Capt Foretop
Burridge, C.	Corporal (RMA)
Chaplin, W.	Private
Chapman, G.	Quartermaster
Christian, J.	Ord
Churchill, C.	AB
Coller, A.	Ord
Costello, J.	Capt Maintop
Couth, C.	AB
Crispin, W.	Private
Daniels, E.	Ldg Seaman
Delbridge, L.	Colour Sergeant
Eckley, J.	AB
Edwards, R.	Asst Surgeon
Ellis, J. W.	Ord
Farlow, E.	AB
Fisher, J. P.	Capt Maintop
Garforth, E. St J.	Lieutenant
Garnett, W. E.	Midshipman
Gibbs, J. C.	AB
Gibson, J.	Gunner's Mate
Gibson, R.	Sergeant (RMA)
Gillen, W.	Private
Gough, A.	Gunner's Mate
Graham, T. V.	AB
Griffin, R. H.	AB
Guillier, R. W.	AB
Gum, G.	Gunner (RMA)
Guret, G. W.	Boy
Hammond, T.	AB
Hannaford, W. T.	AB
Harradon, W. J.	Private
Hartridge, D.	Gunner (RMA)
Hobday, E.	AB
Hocking, W.	AB
Hodge, P.	Private
Hoskin, W. M. G.	Caulker

Hotham, C. F.	Midshipman
Hough, J.	AB
Humby, T.	AB
Humphries, W.	Capt Forecastle
Jago, T.	Ord
Jenkins, S.	AB
Kelly, E.	Lieutenant
Laundry, W.	AB
Lobb, W.	Boatswain's Mate
McDonald, D.	Gunner's Mate
Maitland, J.	Private
Mansfield, A.	Gunner (RMA)
Mansfield, H.	Corporal
Minshall, J. W.	AB
Moorman, F. C.	AB
Morris, J. W. H. C. G.	Lieutenant (RMA)
Mortley, W.	Ord
Mugridge, W.	AB
Nichols, J.	Captain's Cox
Northcott, J.	Private
Oakes, J.	Gunner (RMA)
O'Berry, R.	Ropemaker
Osborne, E.	Gunner (RMA)
Parish, R. W.	Secretary
Pearne, C. H.	Carpenter's Crew
Poole, C.	Ord
Potter, J.	Ldg Seaman
Pound, E.	Ord
Povey, A.	Ord
Putt, J.	Private
Rid, W.	AB
Riordan, M.	AB
Robinson, T.	Ord
Rowland, W.	Private
Ryder, W.	Ord
Saunders, J.	Gunner (RMA)
Scott, J.	Gunner
Seard, J.	Boatswain's Mate
*Seymour, F. B. P.	Commodore
Shore, T.	Captain's Cox
Spriddell, J.	AB
Strong, J.	Private
Sullivan, T.	Capt of Mast
Townsend, J.	AB
Tremlett, J.	AB
Tuckerman, J.	Ldg Seaman
Turner, G.	AB
Veale, J. P.	Boatswain's Mate
Vine, J.	Drummer
Vokes, W.	Gunner (RMA)
Wadlow, E. B.	Midshipman
Ward, W.	AB
Warren, R.	Gunner (RMA)
Watson, A.	Capt Foretop
Webb, J.	Private
Wills, T.	AB
Wilson, T.	Capt Afterguard
Woodger, W.	Ldg Seaman
Woodley, T.	Capt Missentop

H.M.C.S. *Victoria*

H.M.C.S. *Victoria* was a Wooden Screw Sloop armed with 13 x 32 pdr guns. Her tonnage was 580 bm and she was built by Young & Magnay at Limehouse and launched in July 1855. She became a survey vessel in 1864. She was sold in August 1894 to W. Marr of Williamstown; she was broken up in August 1895.

Notes on medal roll:
None.

New Zealand Medal for services in H.M.C.S. *Victoria* in 1860–61.

Ashwell, E.	Trimmer
Bonfield, P.	AB
Brett, G.	AB
Collingwood, J.	AB
Cromarty, J.	AB
Davis, M.	Trimmer
Dudley, T.	AB
Dunn, A.	AB
Edmonds, R.	AB
Ford, H.	AB
Graham, C.	Drummer
Hawkins, J.	AB
Hay, J.	AB
Hood, P.	AB
Horn, W.	Mate
Horseley, W.	AB
Jones, W.	AB
Jones, W.	Cook's Mate
Kensington, A.	Capt Foretop
Lawson, A.	AB
Linton, R.	Quartermaster
Locke, E. J.	AB
Long, S.	Quartermaster
Luther, M.	Gunner's Mate
McIntyre, T.	Trimmer
McMyrm, J.	Trimmer
Marey, G.	Stoker
Norman, W. H.	—
Ovenden, J.	Capt Foretop
Parkes, R.	Trimmer
Rees, B.	Stoker
Schrader, J.	AB
Sibbond, W.	AB
Smith, D.	AB
Smith, S.	Boy
Steward, J.	AB
Stroud, A.	AB
Taylor, J.	Ldg Seaman
White, J.	AB
Woods, G.	Lieutenant

Abyssinian War Medal to
The Royal Navy & Royal Marines

Naval Officers employed in Transport Service

Those recipients marked with an * are also to be found on the roll of HMS *Octavia*.

Aldrich, Wm G.	Staff Commander	Magill, Martin	Surgeon
Aylen, Jno F. R.	Navigating Lieutenant	May, Danl J.	Navigating Lieutenant
Baker, Jas F.	Lieutenant	Montero, Bustan	Carpenter's Servant
*Bardin, Geo G.	Act Inspector Machinery	Moon, Henry	Writer
Bolitho, Edwd A.	Lieutenant	O'Connell, Jno G.	Lieutenant
Boughey, Wm F.	Lieutenant	*Noted on roll as Storekeeper*	
*Bowling, Thos H. L.	Paymaster	Odam, John	Writer
Noted on roll as Secretary to Captain		Parkinson, Chas	Navigating Lieutenant
Brown, Geo S.	Lieutenant	Parks, Murray T.	Lieutenant
*Campbell, J.	Sick Berth Steward	Rainier, Geo H.	Lieutenant
*Childers, W. H.	Lieutenant	Scudamore, John E.	Navigating Lieutenant
Noted on roll as Assistant R.T.O.		*Shaw, Francis G.	Lieutenant
*Coleman, Alfred	Ward Room Officer's Servant	Shuckburgh, Wm C.	Lieutenant
*Cousins, John	Servant (to Mr Bardon)	Stuart, Benjn B.	Staff Commander
*Firth, Thos N.	Paymaster	*Sturgess, Richd	Staff Commander
Noted on roll as Assistant to Insp. Machinery		Sulivan, Thos E.	Lieutenant
*Gillard, Robt	Captain's Steward	Symons, John	Staff Commander
Gilpin, Robt	Navigating Lieutenant	Tryon, Geo	Captain
Going, Philip	Staff Commander	*Principal Officer of Transport Service*	
*Goodwin, Thos E.	Assistant Paymaster	*Warn, Saml	Carpenter
Green, Edmd L.	Lieutenant	Watts, Alfd A. T.	Lieutenant
Hains, Wm P.	Staff Commander	Wise, Chas J.	Lieutenant
Irvine, Jno D'A.	Lieutenant	Wise, Edwin	Navigating Lieutenant
Lewis, Fredk W.	Lieutenant		

HMS *Argus*

A Chong	Ward Room Off's Servt	Bright, Robert	Able Seaman
A fair	Lamptrimer	Brown, Geo W.	2nd Capt Maintop
Ah Hoo	Captain's Cook Asst	Brown, Jno	Gunner (RMA)
Alford, Thomas	Boy	Brown, Richard	Ordinary Seaman
Ali loong	Warrant Off's Cook	Callar, Wm	Gunner
Allen, Ezekl	Sick Berth Attendant	Callister, Willm	Leading Seaman
Amon	Ward Room Steward	Carroll, Mattw	Ordinary Seaman
Ansford, George	Boy	Carroll, Raymond H.	Surgeon
Aquin	Gun Room Steward	Champion, Thomas	Ship's Corporal
Assam	Engineer's Cook	Chanway, John	Stoker
Asseen	Ward Room Off's Servt	Cheyney, James	Stoker
A Why	Ward Room Off's Servt	Child, Jas H.	Boatswain's Mate
Baird, Willm B.	Carpenter's Crew	Clarke, Geo R.	Able Seaman
Barnes, Tom	Able Seaman	Colbourne, David	Ordinary Seaman
Barnett, Richd	Able Seaman	Cole, John	Gunner's Mate
Barnett, Robt	Boy	Collins, Geo O.	Boatswain
Batt, Edwd	Stoker	Collins, Joshua	Ordinary Seaman
Beadell, Chas	Ordinary Seaman	Copland, John	Ship's Cook
Beer, James	Gunner (RMA)	Cornelius, Willm	Ordinary Seaman
Bennett, Chas	Ward Room Cook	Costin, Willm J.	Stoker
Bennett, Geo	Able Seaman	Cowan, Willm	Ordinary Seaman
Blackman, Willm	Ordinary Seaman	Craigh, Tim	Ordinary Seaman

Cresswell, Philip E.	Midshipman
Crisp, Alfd J.	Carpenter's Crew
Critchell, Thomas	Stoker
Crow, Jesse	Carpenter's Crew
Curveth, Rd J.	Boatswain's Mate
Dashwood, Willm	Capt Forecastle
Davis, John	Private
Day, George	Private
Dormer, James	Ordinary Seaman
Duplicate medal sent 22 June 1886	
Driscoll, Willm S.	Able Seaman
Dunn, John	Blacksmith
Edwards, James	Stoker
Errington, Thomas	Ordinary Seaman
Evans, Robt H.	Yeoman of Storerooms
Ewings, James	Stoker
Farrant, John	2nd Capt Afterguard
Fellowes, Wm J.	Assistant Engineer
Ferbrocke, Peter	Boy
Fitzgibbon, Danl	Able Seaman
Ford, Saml	Boy
Fowels, James	Ship's Steward Boy
Fuller, Chas	Ordinary Seaman
Gait, John	Captain's Steward
Galbraith, John	Engineer
Gammon, George	Stoker
Gill, John W.	Boy
Griffin, Richd	Quartermaster
Groves, Wm J.	Boy
Guest, James	Able Seaman
Hallowes, Fredk W.	Commander
Hammond, George	2nd Capt Foretop
Harris, Joseph	Ordinary Seaman
Hawkins, Jno J. P.	Able Seaman
Hewitt, William	Ordinary Seaman
Hill, Ephraim	Gunner (RMA)
Hill, William	Ordinary Seaman
Holt, Edward	Private
Hong	Ward Room Servant
House, Jas A.	Ordinary Seaman
Hughes, William	Ordinary Seaman
Humphreys, Edwd J.	Assistant Engineer
Humphreys, Wm B.	Cooper
Inman, Wm B.	Assistant Paymaster
Isles, Geo E.	Stoker
James, George	Ordinary Seaman
James, Wm H.	Navigating Lieutenant
Jardine, John	Gunner (RMA)
Johns, Henry	Ordinary Seaman
Katesmark, Willm	Boy
Keefe, Alexdr	Quartermaster
Kim Kee	Captain's Cook
Kinder, Ernest	Midshipman
King, Edwd	Stoker
Laughlin, Corns	Stoker
Lawrence, James	Sailmaker's Mate
Le Cornue, Philip	Boy
Lee, William	Leading Stoker
Lindsay, Robt	AB
McFarlane, Thomas	Leading Stoker
Mariner, John	Gun Room Cook
Martins, Robert	Able Seaman
Matthews, George	2nd Capt Maintop
May, Corns	Boy
Meaby, George	Warrant Officer's Servt
Milne, Chas	Midshipman
Money, Sho	Engineer's Servant
Moore, Thos J.	Stoker
Moorman, Isaac B.	Paymaster
Munster, Thomas	Private
Murphy, Dennis	Gunner (RMA)
Murphy, Nichs	Boy
Murray, Hugh	Ordinary Seaman
Murray, W. F.	Lieutenant
Nicholls, Edward	Stoker
Nightingale, Arthur	Boy
Ogle, Robert B. E.	Midshipman
Parks, Henry	Able Seaman
Pearce, Edwd	Able Seaman
Peden, Edward	Quartermaster
Pelly, John H.	Midshipman
Perkin, John	Gun Room Servant
Perrin, William	2nd Capt Foretop .
Pitman, Charles	Boy
Pope, John	Boy
Duplicate medal sent 13 Jan 1914	
Purchase, John	Painter
Read, George E.	Stoker
Rich, James	Ordinary Seaman
Roberts, John	Chief Engineer
Roberts, Sydney	Midshipman
Robilliard, George	Boy
Rogers, Charles	Captain's Coxwain
Ross, William	Able Seaman
Rowe, Geo W.	Able Seaman
Rowell, Robert	Ordinary Seaman
Russell, John	Stoker
Russell, Robert	Stoker
Ryder, James	Sergeant (RMLI)
Saxon, John	Private
Sayce, Rd M.	Midshipman
Sheehan, Bartw	Private
Shepperd, Alexdr	Able Seaman
Shield, George	Assistant Paymaster
Shier, Geo	Ordinary Seaman
Simmonds, Geo	Stoker
Skimming, Willm	Leading Seaman
Sliney, James	Boy
Smith, Archd	Armourer's Crew
Smith, David	Private
Smith, John M.	Drummer (RM)
Smyth, Robt	Ordinary Seaman
Stewart, Wm J. P.	Able Seaman
Stone, John N.	Assistant Surgeon

Swatton, Edwd	Able Seaman
Thomas, John	Leading Stoker
Tippett, John	Able Seaman
Travis, James	Stoker
Tregidgs, Wm H.	Caulker
Triggs, Herbert	Musician
Tyrwhitt, Philip N.	Lieutenant
Waldon, James	Leading Seaman
Way, John	2nd Capt Afterguard
Wells, Henry	Private
West, Robert	Private
Wey, Thomas	Ship's Steward
Williams, John E.	Ordinary Seaman

Williamson, Archd	Ordinary Seaman
Winscom, Saml	Boy
Witehill, Robert	Acting Bombardier
Woodland, Saml	Private
Woodruffe, Richd	Private
Wooldridge, Henry	Leading Seaman
Wright, Robert	Ordinary Seaman
Wyatt, Chas	Carpenter

Returned Medals

Asam	Ward Room Off's Servant
Beardmore, Henry	Private
Loan, Adam	Leading Stoker

H.M.S. *Daphne*

Acklom, Edwin D.	Lieutenant
Adams, Alfred	Boy
Amery, Jas H.	2nd Capt Afterguard
Anderson, James	Ordinary Seaman
Arbert, Geo	Private
Arigus, Jas	Stoker
Arthur, Richard	Musician
Ashwick, Geo F.	Captain's Cook
Baldwin, Henry	Ordinary Seaman
Baldwin, Henry	Boy
Balmen, Thomas	Boatswain's Mate
Barham, Henry	Ordinary Seaman
Barnhouse, Philip	Private
Bartlett, Saml	Ship's Cook
Bascombe, James W. G.	Clerk
Bates, William	Able Seaman
Beer, Fredk G.	Boy
Bennett, Joseph	Ward Room Steward
Bennett, William	Leading Stoker
Bickford, Willm G.	Sailmaker
Blackman, Chas	Quartermaster
Bolt, John	Carpenter's Crew
Borg, Carmeto	Cooper
Bowling, George	Ordinary Seaman
Braby, James (or Brady)	2nd Capt Maintop
Braham, Henry A.	Ordinary Seaman
Brazier, Thomas H.	Painter
Breen, Wm J. P.	Naval Cadet
Broad, Peter	Stoker
Bryan, Henry	Gunner (RMA)
Bull, John	Head Krooman
Burke, William	Ordinary Seaman
Burns, Martin	Gunner (RMA)
Cade, Edward	Gun Room Steward

Duplicate medal sent 31 May 1889

Cardell, Willm H.	Able Seaman
Carpenter, Henry	Gunner (RMA)
Charm, Willm	Private
Chudley, Charles	Private
Churcher, Stephen	Ordinary Seaman
Coles, Richard	Boy

Colley, Henry	Stoker
Cooper, Henry	Chief Engineer
Cox, Walter F.	Boy
Curran, William	Stoker
Davies, George G.	Caulker
Davis, James	Bombardier
Delbridge, Chas	Ship's Steward Boy
Dennis, Willm H.	Boy
Dixon, Robert	Engineer
Doller, Edwin	Able Seaman
Dougall, F. H.	Gunner (RMA)
Dubber, Stephen	Ordinary Seaman
Dullforce, John	Ward Room Off Servant
Dungey, Jas H.	Able Seaman
During, Saml	Warrant Off's Servant
Ecclestone, John	2nd Capt Afterguard
Edwards, John	Midshipman
Evans, George	Boy
Evans, James S.	Shipwright
Falkener, William	Private
Ford, John	Stoker
Ford, John	Private
Freeman, Alfred	2nd Capt Foretop
Gaden, Henry	Able Seaman

Duplicate medal sent 17 May 1870

Gardner, Alan F.	Lieutenant
George, Jimmy	Krooman
Gilbert, Francis	Carpenter's Crew
Glanville, Fredk	Able Seaman
Glass, George	Drummer
Goodyear, Thos H.	Assist Engineer
Grigg, Gifford	Ward Room Off Servant
Halling, Saml	Sick Berth Attendant
Hancock, Willm N.	Able Seaman
Harding, John	Gunner
Harris, James	Stoker

Duplicate medal sent 8 Dec 1885

Haw, William	Sub Lieutenant
Hayward, James	Able Seaman
Heywood, Chas	Boy
Hicks, Simon	2nd Capt Maintop
Hill, Ambrose	Boy

Hill, Willm H. F.	Colour Sergeant	Rounsevell, Sl	Private
Hingston, Alfred	Armourer's Crew	Rowley, Benjn	Able Seaman
Hinn, William	Sub Lieutenant	Samson, John	Leading Seaman
Hiscock, Saml	Leading Stoker	Saunders, Henry	Boy
Hislop, Thomas	Gunner (RMA)	Sauvarin, Peter	Able Seaman
Holsgrove, Frank	Able Seaman	Savey, Jack	Krooman
Hopper, Edwin H.	Ship's Steward	Scott, George	Quartermaster
Hubble, George A.	Able Seaman	Scott, Willm H.	Stoker
Hurrex, Thomas	Ordinary Seaman	Short, Wm H.	2nd Capt Forecastle
Jenkins, George	Engineer's Cook	Silvers, William	Ordinary Seaman
Johnson, Ben	Krooman	Sims, Fredk	Stoker
Joynson, Thomas	Paymaster	Smale, William	Private
Kaford, Henry W.	Able Seaman	Smith, Geo Willm	Able Seaman
Kellar, James J.	Able Seaman	Spencer, Arthur	Boy
Lambert, James	Ordinary Seaman	Stephens, William	Carpenter's Crew
Latteo, Henry	Capt Forecastle	Stevenson, John	2nd Capt Foretop
Lee, Thomas	Able Seaman	Stockham, Henry	Private
Letten, William	Blacksmith	Stuart, Chas C.	Midshipman
McCoy, Joseph	Able Seaman	Sulivan, Geo L.	Commander
McDonald, Henry	Boy	Sullivan, John	Ship's Cook
McKenzie, John	Captain's Steward	Sullivan, Michl	Ordinary Seaman
Duplicate medal sent 19 June 1902		Swanton, R.	Able Seaman
Madge, William	Ward Room Off's Cook	Tall, Aaron	Private
Maguire, Chas E.	Ordinary Seaman	Taplin, Walter	Leading Stoker
Mahony, John	Ordinary Seaman	Tatem, John	Captain's Coxswain
Male, Edwd	Stoker	Taylor, John	Gun Room Steward
Maney, Gay	Krooman	Thompson, John	Private
Martin, John	Boy	Thorn, Willm H.	Ward Room Off's Servant
Matthews, James	Able Seaman	Trafford, Edmd J.	Midshipman
Mellie, Michl	Boy	Vineer, Geo	Able Seaman
Merrett, William	Private	Walker, Henry	Engineer's Servant
Mills, Charles	Leading Stoker	Walters, James	Ship's Corporal
Mole, George	Gunner's Mate	Ward, Fredk	Stoker
Mortimer, Edwd T.	Surgeon	Ward, Willm P.	Engineer
Munday, Thos B.	Boatswain	Watt, R. W.	Midshipman
Murphy, Joseph	Able Seaman	White, George	Navigating Lieutenant
Nicholls, Thomas	Boy	Will, Tom	2nd Head Krooman
Nimrod, John	Krooman	Wills, Thomas	Ordinary Seaman
O'Neill, George	Boy	Wilson, James	Leading Seaman
Orchard, George	Ordinary Seaman	Woodbridge, Albert	Boy 1st class
Osborne, William	Ordinary Seaman	*Duplicate medal sent 27 Nov 1885*	
Peters, James	Able Seaman	Woolby, Thos W.	Warrant Officer's Cook
Pitt, William	Ordinary Seaman	Young, George	Ordinary Seaman
Price, Edwd	Boy		
Priddy, Chas J.	Ordinary Seaman		
Pugh, Willm H.	Boatswain's Mate	*Returned Medals*	
Rendle, Chas H. C.	Able Seaman	Coffey, Peter	Private
Richards, James	Carpenter	Creeper, Tom	Krooman
Ross, John	Stoker	Routledge, William	Captain's Cook Assistant

H.M.S. *Dryad*

Allen, Geo W.	Senior Lieutenant	Blake, Henry	Boy 1st class
Allen, William	Sailmaker's Mate	Blight, William	Ward Room Steward
Anson, John	Leading Seaman	Bonney, Saml	Stoker 2nd class
Ashman, Thos	Private	Boteler, Hy H.	Midshipman
Barlow, John	Ordinary Seaman	Brown, Fredk H.	Boy
Bawtree, Edward J.	Midshipman	Brown, Fredk W.	Chief Engineer

Bunker, Saml	Carpenter's Crew
Butcher, Edmund	Boy
Butcher, William	Ward Room Cook
Callaghan, John	Private
Canham, Willm	Ordinary Seaman
Carter, George	Stoker
Caulfield, Richd	Leading Seaman
Clarke, James	Ordinary Seaman
Clarke, Norman L. H.	Sub Lieutenant
Clements, Edwin	Ordinary Seaman
Cogan, John	Warrant Off's Cook
Coleman, Edwd	Able Seaman
Coleman, Geo D.	Able Seaman
Coombes, John	Ordinary Seaman
Cove, Richd	Cooper
Cryer, Alfred	Ordinary Seaman
Curnow, Josh	Painter
Curtis, Emanuel T.	Ordinary Seaman
Dabner, Thos	Ordinary Seaman
Dale, Wm	Boy
Dally, George	Private

Duplicate medal sent 20 May 1900

Darton, Thos	Ship's Cook
Deidum, Frank	Able Seaman
Devine, John	Quartermaster
Dunbar, Robt	Gunner (RMA)
Dyer, John	Private
Edwards, Wm	2nd Capt Afterguard
Elliott, Joseph	Ordinary Seaman
Feabes, Henry	2nd Capt Foretop
Fellowes, Thos H. B.	Commander
Fielder, Henry J.	Ordinary Seaman
Foley, John	Able Seaman
Fox, John	Gunner (RMA)
Giles, Christ	Ordinary Seaman
Gillday, Patk	Gunner (RMA)
Gillett, Solomon	2nd Capt Afterguard
Good, Fredk C.	Clerk

Duplicate medal sent 8 October 1872

Greenwood, James	Ordinary Seaman
Grundry, Josh	Captain's Cook
Habakkuk, Wm	Sailmaker's Crew
Hancock, William	Stoker
Harrington, Danl	Ordinary Seaman
Hawkeswood, Wm	Boy
Hawkins, Chas	Stoker
Haydon, James	Boy
Hayward, Wm H.	Navigating Lieutenant
Hile, Thos J.	Boy
Hodge, Chas W.	Ordinary Seaman
Hodge, Richd	Capt Forecastle
Honeychurch, Nichs	Able Seaman
Hoskin, Josiah	Ordinary Seaman
Husbands, Wm	Stoker
Husk, Wm H.	Ordinary Seaman
Jackson, Robt	2nd Capt Maintop
Jarvis, George	Private

Duplicate medal sent 21 May 1873

Jeffrey, Joseph	Private
Johns, Henry A.	Carpenter
Keast, Geo A.	Ward Room
Keogh, Michl	Stoker
Kinsman, Chas	Able Seaman
Lawrence, Edwd	Ordinary Seaman
Leach, John	Stoker
Lean, John	Stoker
Ledan, Henry	Armourer's Crew
Lewis, John	Private
Luxmore, James	Gun Room Cook
Madge, John	Acting Corporal (RM)
Marsh, William	Caulker
Martin, James	Boy
Matthews, Job	Leading Seaman
Maxwell, Wm H.	Commander
May, Nicholas	Engineer's Servant
Medlon, Wm G.	Colour Sergeant (RM)
Miles, Henry	Gunner (RMA)
Milford, Saml	Stoker
Morrow, Richd	Ordinary Seaman
Nance, Thos	Boy

Duplicate medal sent 16 June 1908

Netting, Richd	Boatswain
Nettleton, Edwd	Ship's Steward
Nicolson, Chas A.	Lieutenant
Noble, Fredk C.	Ordinary Seaman
Noonan, Wm	Able Seaman
O'Connor, Danl	Surgeon
Osmond, Wm	Quartermaster
Parker, Fredk	Paymaster
Paxton, Timy	Private
Payne, John	Stoker
Pendleton, Fredk T.	Engineer
Pengelly, Benjn	Able Seaman
Perryman, Geo T.	Boatswain's Mate
Pillar, John	Boy
Pitcher, John	Captain's Coxwain
Power, John	Boy
Quinn, Wm J.	Blacksmith's Apprentice
Renfrey, John C.	Caulker's Apprentice
Roberts, James	Ordinary Seaman
Roberts, Richd H.	Ordinary Seaman
Robinson, Saml	Gunner's Mate
Sellick, Robt	Private
Sergeroet, Justin	Captain's Steward
Settle, Fredk	Warrant Off's Servant
Shearer, Saml	Ward Room Off's Servant
Shears, Wm	Carpenter's Mate
Shilston, John	Sick Berth Attendant
Skerritt, Wm	Private
Slade, Robt	Engineer's Cook
Slade, Robt G.	Carpenter's Crew
Smeaton, James	Stoker
Smith, George	Ward Room Off's Servant
Smith, Robert	Gunner's Mate
Sprague, Thos	Stoker

Stanford, Wm	Stoker	Vickery, George	2nd Capt Foretop
Steer, William	Ordinary Seaman	Wakeham, Richd K.	Boy
Stewart, Chas B.	Gun Room Steward	Wall, James	Ship's Steward Assistant
Symons, Thos	Ship's Corporal	Walters, Joseph	Chief Cook's Assistant
Tapley, Wm	Blacksmith	*Duplicate medal sent 23 February 1922*	
Thewey, James	Stoker	Wells, Jas W. W.	Midshipman
Thompson, Danl	Boy	Wilkie, William	Gunner
Thompson, Thos	Leading Stoker	Williams, David	Leading Stoker
Thompson, Wm	Musician	Williams, John P.	Assistant Engineer
Tickle, Thos	Leading Stoker	Williams, Thomas	Gunner (RMA)
Trebilcock, Fras	Ordinary Seaman	Windham, Chas	Midshipman
Tregenna, Richd	Assistant Engineer	Winter, Joseph	Able Seaman
Turner, John	2nd Capt Forecastle	Woodbridge, William	2nd Capt Maintop
Twiss, Wm	Private		
Vallack, Alfred	Ordinary Seaman		
Duplicate medal sent 12 December 1911		*Returned Medal*	
Vaughan, Thos	Boatswain's Mate	Ford, John	Boy

HMS *Nymph*

Allen, James	Able Seaman	Craddock, George J.	Assistant Engineer
Alton, John	Private	Cranries, Philip	Stoker
Anderson, William	Boy	Croot, William	Boy
Ashby, Josh	Boatswain's Mate	Dalby, Amos	Boy
Avery, John	Boy	Darrington, Samuel	Private
Babbs, Thomas	Able Seaman	Davey, Charles	2nd Capt Forecastle
Baker, Israel E.	Gunner (RMA)	Davis, William	Able Seaman
Ball, Edwin C.	Able Seaman	Death, William	Ordinary Seaman
Ball, Thomas	Engineer's Cook	Dollimore, Joseph	Able Seaman
Baptist, John	Engineer's Cook	Dorey, George	Gunner (RMA)
(alias J. Baptiste De Souza)		Duller, William	2nd Capt Afterguard
Barnardiston, Thomas	Commander	Dulley, Henry G.	Able Seaman
Barogan, James	Ordinary Seaman	Dyer, Samuel	Leading Stoker
Barry, Patrick	Boatswain	Dyer, Willm J.	Armourer's Crew
Barton, James	Ordinary Seaman	Elliker, Richard	Captain's Steward
Batchelor, George	Ward Room Off Servant	Ellis, Alexander	Gunner
Bath, George	Able Seaman	Fegheley, Henry	Private
Bell, Danl	Able Seaman	Fitzgerald, Thomas	Able Seaman
Biddlecombe, George	Able Seaman	Foster, Charles	Ordinary Seaman
Bissell, Alfred	Sergeant (RM)	Freeman, Tom	Krooman
Bourne, William	Stoker	Fretter, Edwd J.	Sailmaker's Mate
Bromilow, Francis R.	Lieutenant	Full, Joseph	Boy
Brown, Jim	Krooman	Fuller, John	Ward Room Off Servant
Brown, Tom	Head Krooman	Gascoigne, John	Shipwright
Bryant, John	Capt Forecastle	Gascoigne, Thomas	Gunner (RMA)
Burge, William	Able Seaman	Gemmell, William	Ordinary Seaman
Burnham, Charles	Ordinary Seaman	George, Fredk	Stoker
Butcher, John	Private	George, King	Krooman
Cain, Thomas	Ship's Cook	George, Thomas	2nd Capt Foretop
Callaghan, Eugene	Ordinary Seaman	Gillate, Christr	Ordinary Seaman
Carpenter, Henry J.	Ordinary Seaman	Goodall, Joseph	Engineer's Servant
Caton, Mathw W.	Stoker	Graham, Edwd	2nd Capt Afterguard
Caulker, Charles	Ward Room Off Servant	Gready, Michl	Sick Berth Attendant
Challice, John A.	Lieutenant	Grey, John	Stoker
Chapman, Francis H.	Senior Lieutenant	Gribble, George	Able Seaman
Charlie, Tom	Krooman	Gulley, Samuel	Able Seaman
Chisnell, Robert E.	Assistant Engineer	Guy, Henry	Gunner's Mate
Cooper, Edwd J.	Ship's Steward	Halley, John	Private

Hamond, Douglas	Naval Cadet & Midshipman	Parson, Philip A.	Midshipman
Harrington, Thomas J.	Boy	Peters, John	Gunner (RMA)
Hassan, Mahomet	Interpreter	Peterson, Thomas	Boatswain's Mate
Hayes, Michael	Quartermaster	Phillips, David	Able Seaman
Heath, Thomas F.	Leading Seaman	Pike, James	2nd Capt Maintop
Hibbert, Henry	Stoker	Plant, Richard	Boy
Hill, George	Sailmaker's Crew	Radford, Edgar	Clerk
Hines, Fredk	Able Seaman	Randall, James	Blacksmith
Hirtzel, George J.	Navigating Lieutenant	Randell, John G.	Captain's Coxwain
Hodge, Thomas B.	Boy	Ridge, George	Boy
Hodgson, Thomas J.	Sub Lieutenant	Rogers, Henry	Ordinary Seaman
Hopkins, Chas H.	Navigating Sub Lieutenant	Ross, William	Engineer
Hoskin, James R.	Carpenter's Crew	Royal, Abraham	Private
Hudson, Michl	Private	Ryan, Edward	Warrant Officer's Servant
Jeandron, James	Ordinary Seaman	Rynard, Chas E.	Midshipman
Johnson, William	Stoker	Scarrott, Thomas	Stoker
Johnson, William	Corporal (RMA)	Sherry, George	Gunner's Mate
Johnston, Thomas E.	Stoker	Smart, Jack	Krooman
Joyce, Henry	Ordinary Seaman	Smith, Alfred	Engineer
Kelly, Philip	Ordinary Seaman	Smith, Fredk H.	Warrant Officer's Servant
Kest, Arthur	Ordinary Seaman	Smith, George	Gun Room Cook
King, Tom	Krooman	Smith, Henry	Ward Room Servant
Laporte, Richd de	Musician	Smith, Joseph	2nd Capt Foretop
Lee, John	Gunner (RMA)	Stafford, Joseph	Ordinary Seaman
Leech, David	Warrant Officer's Cook	Staunton, Richard	Carpenter's Crew
Lewis, William	Chief Engineer	Taylor, Alfred C.	Stoker
Livingstone, Dug	Leading Stoker	Taylor, George	Ordinary Seaman
Maccall, Alex V.	Paymaster	Thomas, Joseph	Captain's Cook
Machine, Josiah B.	Ordinary Seaman	Thomlin, Thomas	Leading Stoker
McGuire, John	Gunner (RMA)	Toyer, Alfred J.	Cooper's Crew
Mansergh, Richard W.	Midshipman	Tyrrell, Geo J.	Boy
Mason, Charles	Leading Stoker	Vall, Vady	Ward Room Cook
Mason, John L.	Carpenter	Warner, John	Able Seaman
Matthews, William	Stoker	Weeden, Richard	Private
Maxwell, Thomas E.	Midshipman	Westmoreland, John	Stoker
Miller, John J.	Boy	Weston, Joseph	Quartermaster
Mitchell, William	Able Seaman	White, Thomas	Private
Mortimer, William	Ordinary Seaman	Whitehead, Willm J.	Able Seaman
Murphy, James	Able Seaman	Williams, James	Able Seaman
Nevin, Patk	Leading Seaman	*(alias Hy Richards)*	
Newman, Arthur	Captain's Cook Assistant	Wilson, William	Gunner (RMA)
Nicklin, Fredk	Ordinary Seaman	Winsor, Thos L.	Boy
Noble, John	Surgeon	Wytralingam, Rattam	Gun Room Steward
Nokes, Fredk	Leading Seaman	Yale, John	Leading Stoker
Norman, William	Boy		
Norris, James	Stoker		
Owen, Gronwy	Carpenter's Crew	*Returned medals*	
Palmer, Thomas	Ship's Steward Boy	Doyle, Patrick	Private
Parker, Henry	Able Seaman	Johnson, Ben	2nd Head Krooman

HMS *Octavia*

Abbott, Henry	Painter	Alexander, William	Ordinary Seaman
Duplicate medal sent 7 Nov 1873		Allen, Amos	Armourer
Abbott, Samuel	Boy	Allport, William	Stoker
Aiken, John	Private	Anderson, William	Stoker
Aishton, John	Blacksmith	Andrew, Dick	Krooman
Allames, Thomas	Private	Arnold, William	Gun Room Steward

Ashpole, Richard	Private	Boyce, William	Able Seaman
Ashton, Thomas	Warrant Off's Servant	Bradshaw, Samuel	Leading Seaman
Atkins, Arthur	Boy	Brard, William	Carpenter's Crew
Atkinson, George L.	Sub Lieutenant	Britten, Walter	Stoker
Attwell, Richard	Ordinary Seaman	*Duplicate medal sent to party 16.6.09*	
Attwells, Samuel	Plumber	Broganza, Louis	Ward Room Off's Servant
Austin, Charles	2nd Capt Foretop	Brooke, Gerard M.	Midshipman
Austin, William	Able Seaman	Brooks, Adam	Bandsman
Avery, William H.	Able Seaman	Brooks, Eugene	Boy
Ayers, William	Bandsman	Brown, Charles	Able Seaman
Babbage, William N.	Private	Brown, Edward	Able Seaman
Bain, Morris	Gunner	Brown, John	Ordinary Seaman
Baker, James	Ship's Cook	Brown, John	Ordinary Seaman
Baker, John W.	Private	Brown, Michael	Leading Seaman
Bardin, George G.	Act Inspector Machinery	Bruce, Walter	Painter
Barker, Henry A.	Leading Seaman	Brunton, Henry S.	Boy
Barkley, Charles	Able Seaman	Buckle, Charles J.	Carpenter
Barkley, James	Able Seaman	Bull, Edward	Stoker
Barnard, Edward M.	Ship's Steward	Bullen, Robert H.	Paymaster
Barnes, Joe	Ordinary Seaman	Burden, John	Ordinary Seaman
Barnes, John	Private	Butler, John	Capt Maintop
Barnes, William	Able Seaman	Campbell, Colin A.	Captain
Barnett, Daniel	Ordinary Seaman	Campbell, James	Sick Berth Steward
Bartley, James	Private	Cann, George	Warrant Off's Cook
Bates, James A.	Able Seaman	Carpenter, James	Stoker
Bates, John F.	Ordinary Seaman	Carr, John J.	Able Seaman
Baylis, William	Able Seaman	Carr, William	Capt Foretop
Beard, David D.	Able Seaman	Carroll, John	Gunner
Beatty, James	Capt Mast	Carson, Robert	Coxwain Cutter
Beavis, Joshua	Quartermaster	Casey, James	Able Seaman
Bennett, George	Able Seaman	Chainey, Thomas	Ship's Corporal
Benstead, James	Leading Seaman	Challey, George	Private
Best, James	Able Seaman	Chambers, Thomas	Private
Betts, William	Midshipman	Chapman, George S.	Ordinary Seaman
Bevan, Lambton L.	Lieutenant	Chapman, James	Ordinary Seaman
Bewicke, Calverley T.	Act Sub Lieutenant	Chard, William	Ordinary Seaman
Bidgood, George	Boatswain's Mate	Childers, William H.	Lieutenant
Bigger, Robert	Ordinary Seaman	Chillingworth, Edward	Able Seaman
Biggs, Henry	Private	Chinn, Henry	Able Seaman
Bigwood, Godfrey	Ordinary Seaman	Churchard, Edward	Tinsmith
Bird, George	Stoker	Churchill, Joseph	Boy
Bishop, Alfred	Able Seaman	Clair, Henry	Able Seaman
Blaby, Richard	Capt Forecastle	Clarke, Arthur C.	Act Sub Lieutenant
Bladon, Joshua	Leading Seaman	Clarke, Edward W.	Ordinary Seaman
Blake, James	Stoker	Clarke, George	Able Seaman
Bleach, John W.	Ordinary Seaman	Clarke, James	Chief Stoker
Bogan, James	Leading Seaman	Clarke, William	Ordinary Seaman
Bohane, Michael	Ordinary Seaman	Clayton, George F.	Able Seaman
Boobier, John	Boy	Clements, John	Ordinary Seaman
Border, John	Leading Seaman	Clift, William H.	Boy
Bowden, Thomas	Private	Cock, Charles	Clerk
Bowen, Edwin	Armourer	Coffee, Tom	Head Krooman
Bowers, William S.	Shipwright	Coker, John	Able Seaman
Bowler, David	Boy	Cole, George	Able Seaman
Bowling, Thomas H. L.	Paymaster	Coleman, Alfred	Ward Room Off's Servant
Bowman, Thomas S.	Ordinary Seaman	Colenutt, John	Capt Forecastle
Boxer, William E.	Asst Paymaster	Collins, Frederick	Able Seaman

Collins, George	Ordinary Seaman
Collins, Jas R.	Ordinary Seaman
Collins, Robert	Able Seaman
Connell, James	Lamp Trimmer
Conner, Hugh	Able Seaman
Cook, George	Boatswain's Mate
Coombs, Richard	Stoker
Cooper, William	Cook's Mate
Court, Dudley	Midshipman
Courtnell, Frederick	Carpenter's Crew
Cousins, George G.	Able Seaman
Cousins, John *(or Casimiro)*	Servant
Crawford, George	Private
Crievey, Michael	Private
Crockford, Charles	Ordinary Seaman
Crofton, Duke A.	Midshipman
Crook, Benjamin	Ordinary Seaman
Crotty, Thomas	Able Seaman
Croucher, William	Ordinary Seaman
Cummins, Henry A. T.	Clerk
Cutting, William	Private
Daley, James	Ordinary Seaman
Dance, Henry	Private

Appears twice on the medal roll but only one medal appears to have been issued.

Daniells, Jno	Admiral's Coxwain
Daniells, John H.	Ordinary Seaman
Dann, George	Leading Stoker
Davidson, Andrew	Able Seaman
Davie, Matthew	Boy
Davis, Daniel	Quartermaster
Davis, James	Boy
Davis, John	Ordinary Seaman
Deaville, George	Private
Deer, Emanuel C.	Ordinary Seaman
Devlin, John	Able Seaman
Dinnett, John	Stoker
Dockerell, Thomas	Able Seaman
Dockings, William H.	Boatswain
Dodge, Edwin	Boy
Donoghue, John	Ordinary Seaman
Driscoll, William	Able Seaman
Dudridge, Robert	Ordinary Seaman
Duhig, William	Able Seaman
Duley, Charles	Able Seaman
Duncombe, Henry	Cooper's Crew
Dunlop, Softlan	Sailmaker's Mate
Dye, Alfred W.	Able Seaman
Dye, George	Gun Room Steward
Earwicker, William	Able Seaman
Eastman, George	Krooman
Ede, Charles	Boy
Ede, James	Ordinary Seaman
Edgar, Henry J.	Midshipman
Edwards, Charles D.	Ordinary Seaman
Edwards, George	Stoker
Eldridge, Richard	Able Seaman

Elliott, William	Able Seaman
Ellis, Daniel B.	Ordinary Seaman
Ellis, William	Stoker
Elmes, Joseph	Able Seaman
Emsden, Thomas	Able Seaman

Duplicate medal sent to party 22.3.98

Eschrich, George	Bandmaster
Fabry, Powers	Able Seaman
Facey, Peter	Ship's Steward Asst
Fanton, Jno F.	Ordinary Seaman
Ferguson, Alexander H.	Ordinary Seaman
Ferguson, James H.	Engineer
Festing, Edmund G.	Lieutenant
Fiddler, Edward	Boy
Finn, Morris	Sailmaker's Crew
Flanagan, James	Stoker
Flemming, John	Stoker
Fluck, William	Private
Flynn, Patrick	Able Seaman
Flynn, Richard	Able Seaman
Fortune, Mark	Private
Foster, John	Ordinary Seaman

Duplicate medal sent 15 Sept 1892

Foster, John	Private
Fraine, Henry H.	Ordinary Seaman
Fraser, Osborne F. C.	Captain (RMLI)
Frazer, David	Carpenter's Crew
Freeth, Joseph R.	Able Seaman
French, Alfred	Captain's Steward
Frith, Thomas N.	Paymaster
Fry, Thomas	Ordinary Seaman
Fryer, Edward A.	Act/Sub Lieutenant
Full, William	Ward Room Servant
Gale, John	Ship's Cook
Galloway, James H.	Midshipman
Gardener, George P.	Assistant Engineer
Gardner, John	Leading Seaman
Gardner, William H.	Boy
Gemmell, James	Armourer
Gibbons, Joshua	Blacksmith's Crew
Gifford, Thomas	Ordinary Seaman
Giles, George	Ordinary Seaman
Gillard, Robert	Captain's Steward
Glasspole, William	Chief Engineer
Gliddon, John T.	Boy
Godsall, William	Private
Goodburn, John	Boy
Goodchild, William	Ordinary Seaman
Goode, Charles	Private
Goodridge, Walter S.	Midshipman
Goodwin, Thomas E.	Assistant Paymaster
Gorman, Benjamin	Sailmaker
Goss, Joseph	Private
Graham, John	Boatswain's Mate
Gray, George, A.	Ordinary Seaman
Green, John	Boy
Green, Joseph	Stoker
Green, Thomas	Gunner (RMA)

Green, Walter	Boy	Ingram, John	Gunner (RMA)
Gregory, James	Able Seaman	Ings, William	Boy
Gregory, William	Able Seaman	Ireland, Reuben	Able Seaman
Grigg, Matthew	2/Capt Forecastle	Irvine, Jno D'A.	Lieutenant
Groves, Esau	Quartermaster	Jack, William	Ordinary Seaman
Gubandon, William	Ordinary Seaman	Jago, James	Leading Seaman
Hagan, John	Private	Janes, William T.	Ordinary Seaman
Hailes, Thomas	Ordinary Seaman	Jefferies, James A.	Ordinary Seaman
Hale, Edwin	Sergeant (RM)	Jeffery, William	Able Seaman
Harding, James	Ordinary Seaman	Jenkins, Edward	Able Seaman
Harkham, Joseph	Ship's Corporal	Jenkins, William	Gunner
Harkin, Philip	Leading Stoker	Johnston, Edward	Ordinary Seaman
Harris, James	Boy	Jones, Charles H.	Chief Gunner's Mate
Duplicate medal sent to C-in-C Australia		Jones, James	Engineer
for party on 22.5.06		Jones, John	Gunner
Harris, James	Gun Room Steward	Joslin, Henry H.	Private
Harris, John	Asst Sick Berth Attendant	Joyce, Henry	Boy
Harris, John G.	Boy	Keefe, Martin	Stoker
Harris, William	Private	Kemp, Francis R. B.	Lieutenant
Harvey, Thomas	Able Seaman	Kentsbeer, Samuel	Quartermaster
Harvey, Walter	Gunner	Keys, Francis J.	Stoker
Hatt, Mark	Ordinary Seaman	King, David	Ordinary Seaman
Hawkins, John	Private	King, Thomas A.	Chief Boatswain's Mate
Hayden, Charles	Ordinary	King, William	Gunner (RMA)
Haygreen, James H. G.	Private	Kisseck, Alexander	Able Seaman
Hayles, George W.	Carpenter's Crew	Kite, William	Carpenter's Mate
Haylock, Edward	Leading Seaman	Kittle, George	Gunner
Hearn, William	Boatswain's Mate	Knight, Thomas	2/Capt Afterguard
Heath, Sir Leopold G.	Commodore	Knight, Thomas	Sailmaker's Crew
Heggerty, John	Capt Afterguard	Knight, William	Able Seaman
Hele, John J.	Boy	Knowler, Thomas	Ward Room Steward
Hennessey, James	Ordinary Seaman	Lawler, Thomas	Leading Seaman
Hennessey, Thomas	Able Seaman	Lee, Lawrence	Ordinary Seaman
Herbert, Charles	Ordinary Seaman	Leek, George	Boatswain's Mate
Hewett, Robert	Gun Room Cook	Leslie, Robert M.	Boy
Hewitt, James	Able Seaman	Lever, John	Gunner
Hile, Henry J.	Boy	Levett, Thomas	Musician
Hill, George	Ordinary Seaman	Lewis, Sam	Krooman
Hill, William M. T.	Able Seaman	Light, Richard	Leading Seaman
Hilton, James	Yeoman Signals	Lihou, Peter	Boy
Hipwell, William H.	Boy	*Duplicate medal sent to party 15.4.13*	
Hoar, Charles	Leading Seaman	Lilly, Thomas	Ship's Corporal
Hodder, Joseph G.	Boy	Lloyd, Samuel	Engineer
Hodgson, Thomas	Coxwain Pinnace	Loader, Luke	Ordinary Seaman
Hoey, James	Boy	Lobo, Jerome	Captain's Servant
Holdaway, John	Quartermaster	Lock, Harry	Ward Room Off's Servant
Hookway, James	Private	Lock, John	Boy
Hooper, William	Able Seaman	Louis, Silestian	Commander's Domestic
Hopkins, Henry	Gun Room Steward	Love, William	Carpenter's Mate
Horne, Robert G.	Ordinary Seaman	Lover, Edwin	Engineer's Servant
Howard, Richard	Able Seaman	Lucas, Daniel	Private
Howard, Thomas	Leading Stoker	Lyne, Alfred R.	Ordinary Seaman
Howell, William F.	Ordinary Seaman	Lungley, Frederick J.	Ordinary Seaman
Hudson, William H.	Able Seaman	McConvey, Peter	Able Seaman
Hunter, Alfred	Signalman	McDermott, Charles	Boy
Hutchinson, Albert	Carpenter's Crew	McDonnell, Thomas	Private
Hutchinson, James	Private	Mace, Edward	Able Seaman
Hutton, P. W. P.	Navigating Midshipman	Mace, William	Ward Room Cook

McGowan, Robert	Ordinary Seaman	O'Flaherty, William	Ordinary Seaman
McGowan, William	Able Seaman	O'Neill, John	Able Seaman
McIntosh, Colin	Able Seaman	Orris, Frederick J.	Ordinary Seaman
McLean, Henry	Able Seaman	Owen, John	Able Seaman
McLeod, George	Engineer	Paget, Claude	Midshipman
Maclear, Jno F. P.	Lieutenant	Paisley, Charles D.	Caulker's Mate
McLeod, John	Boy	Parish, William G.	Boy
McQuade, John	Ship's Corporal	*Number 121 on ship's books*	
McNeil, Daniel	Able Seaman	Parish, William G.	Boy
Madden, John	Sailmaker	*Number 475 on ship's books*	
Madden, Thomas	Bandsman	Pawsey, Charles J.	Assistant Paymaster
Magill, Martin	Surgeon	Payne, Charles	Carpenter's Crew
Maitland, Brownlow	Midshipman	Payne, James	Gunner
Mann, James	Bandsman	Payne, William	2/Capt Afterguard
Marsh, Edward	Ordinary Seaman	Pearce, Thomas	Gunner
Marsh, Frederick	Sailmaker's Mate	Pearce, William	Ordinary Seaman
Marshall, John	Gunner	Pearce, William	Stoker
Marshall, Joseph	Ship's Steward Asst	Peer, Robert	Private
Marshman, William	Private	Pelling, George	Boy
Martin, Charles	Stoker	Penrose, Edward C.	Leading Stoker
Masterson, Robert	Able Seaman	Petherick, Thomas	Master-at-Arms
May, Daniel J.	Navigating Lieutenant	Phillips, George	Able Seaman
Mayo, Thomas	Able Seaman	Phillips, Joseph	Able Seaman
Merrett, James	Stoker	Pike, George	Signalman
Millett, Jacob	Sick Berth Steward	Pincom, George	Ordinary Seaman
Milligan, William	Able Seaman	Pinto, Francis	Secretary's Servant
Milmer, John	Able Seaman	Pinto, Louis	Ward Room Off's Servant
Mires, William	Private	Pittis, Charles	2/Capt Forecastle
Mitchell, Charles	Leading Seaman	Pitts, John	Boy
Monally, Michael	Capt Maintop	Pocklington, Arthur J.	Midshipman
Mondey, John	Boy	Pocock, William	Able Seaman
Montero, Bustaro	Ward Room Off's Servant	Poe, Leonard	Capt Hold
Moody, George	Stoker	Poorfellow, Tom	Krooman
Moon, Henry	Writer	Poling, Charles J.	Commodore's Steward
Moore, Jas J.	Able Seaman	Polley, James	Ordinary Seaman
Morgan, James	Private	Porter, Robert	Able Seaman
Morgan, William	Gunner	Pounds, Thomas	Navigating Lieutenant
Morris, Robert	Stoker	Power, Thomas	Leading Seaman
Morse, Robert	Able Seaman	Powles, Edward S.	Chaplain
Mostyn, Hon Evan L. V.	Lieutenant	Pratt, William	Able Seaman
Murphy, Cornelius	Able Seaman	Privett, John	Able Seaman
Myers, Frank	Able Seaman	Quill, Michael	Able Seaman
Myers, Thomas	Ordinary Seaman	Quinton, Thomas	Able Seaman
Myhill, Samuel	Ordinary Seaman	Rama, Kersa	Captain's Cook Assistant
Nadall, William	Ordinary Seaman	Ramsay, John S.	Clerk
Nairn, Andrew	Capt Afterguard	Randell, Charles	Able Seaman
Napier, Hon Basil	Midshipman	Ranssell, Francis	Private
Nash, William H.	Boy	Ratchford, John	Leading Seaman
Neal, Job	Able Seaman	Raven, Robert	Boy
Newman, Edward	Ordinary Seaman	Rawlinson, Joseph	Able Seaman
Nicholls, George	Ordinary Seaman	Read, Henry W.	Sick Berth Steward
Nimbly, Tom	Krooman	Read, John	Able Seaman
Norris, Robert	Ordinary Seaman	Read, William	Gunner's Mate
Nortrupp, George	Private	Rees, William	Boatswain's Mate
Nugent, George A.	Ordinary Seaman	Reeves, John	Leading Stoker
Odam, John	Writer	Remy, John	Capt Mast
O'Donoghue, James	Quartermaster	Richards, Thomas H.	Ordinary Seaman

Ridd, William	Leading Stocker	Snudden, Thomas	Able Seaman
Riggs, John	Able Seaman	Spence, Charles H.	Chief Yeoman Signals
Rittey, John	Boy	Spinks, James	Coxwain Cutter
Rivers, William A.	Able Seaman	Spurling, Samuel W.	Shipwright
Roberts, Anscombe	Able Seaman	Squire, Robert	Corporal (RM)
Roberts, Levi	Gunner (RMA)	Stainsbury, Henry	Private
Roberts, William	Ordinary Seaman	Stanley, Henry	Bandsman
Roberts, William H.	Able Seaman	Stanmore, Robert J.	Boy
Robins, Richard	Gunner	Starling, William J.	Boy
Robinson, John H.	Yeoman Storeroom	Starks, Ben	Coxwain Barge
Robinson, Thomas	Assistant Paymaster	Stembridge, Samuel	Leading Seaman
Robinson, William	Butcher	Stewart, Donald	2/Capt Maintop
Rohss, Oliver A.	Boy	Stone, William H.	Ordinary Seaman
Rogers, Henry	Armourer	Stout, Tom	Krooman
Ronter, Thomas	Rope Maker	Sturgess, Richard	Staff Commander
Rose, James	Gunner (RMA)	Sueza, Antonia de	Bandsman
Rounce, Daniel	Ordinary Seaman	Sueza, Joseph de	Tailor
Rowe, Thomas	Leading Seaman	Sueza, Pedro P. de	Ward Room Off's Servant
Rule, George F. H.	Lieutenant (RMLI)	Summerfield, James	Stoker
Ryan, Matthew F.	Act/Assistant Surgeon	Sunday, Jack	Krooman
Ryder, James	Private	Sweeney, Hugh	Ordinary Seaman
Salter, Isaac	Ordinary Seaman	Sweeney, John	Private
Sanibles, Charles	Stoker	Sykes, Sam	Gunner
Scott, George W.	Bandsman	Taylor, J. R.	Shoemaker
Scott, Henry	Assistant Engineer	Thoburn, William	Private
Scrivens, Frederick	Able Seaman	Thomas, Charles	Able Seaman
Scudder, Walter	Ordinary Seaman	Thomas, Josiah	Krooman
Searle, Thomas	Leading Stoker	Thomas, Thomas	Bombardier
Sedgwick, Henry N. M.	Assistant Surgeon	Thomas, William	Rope Maker
Seymeur, John	Schoolmaster	Tilley, Frederick	Able Seaman
Seymour, Thomas	Leading Seaman	Tom, Long	Krooman
Shalwell, William	Ordinary Seaman	Trapnell, Alfred	Ordinary Seaman
Shanks, Arthur	Engineer	*Duplicate medal sent to party 1.12.1909*	
Shaw, Doyle M.	Surgeon	Tregaskiss, Arthur G.	Act/Navigating Lieut
Shaw, Francis G.	Lieutenant	Triggs, Reuben	Captain's Coxwain
Shea, James	Gunner's Mate	Triggs, William	Ordinary Seaman
Sherlock, James	Ordinary Seaman	Trinder, Henry S.	Boy
Ship, Mike	Cooper	Trotman, William	Boy
Shorter, John	Boatswain's Mate	Trowell, Richard	Boy
Shoud, John	Stoker	Tucker, Edward W.	Carpenter's Crew
Showler, William	Private	Turner, William	Able Seaman
Simmonds, George	Ordinary Seaman	Trussell, Edward	Ordinary Seaman
Simmons, Robert	Able Seaman	Veness, Samuel A.	Able Seaman
Smale, Thomas A.	Carpenter's Crew	Veryard, John J.	Barber
Smith, Alfred	Boy	Vickary, John	Gunner (RMA)
Smith, Charles	Bandsman	Wade, William	Armourer's Crew
Smith, Charles	Ordinary Seaman	Wagner, Christopher	Ordinary Seaman
Smith, Henry	Boy	Walker, Henry C.	Lieutenant
Smith, John	Able Seaman	Wallace, John	Ordinary Seaman
Smith, John	Private	Walton, Thomas	Able Seaman
Smith, Joseph	Able Seaman	Wane, George	Stoker
Smith, Robert C.	Ordinary Seaman	Warman, Dick	2nd Head Krooman
Smith, Walter T.	Ordinary Seaman	Warn, Samuel	Carpenter
Smith, William	Private	Warry, George J.	Able Seaman
Smith, William	Ward Room Off's Servant	Washington, Charles	Ordinary Seaman
Smith, William J.	Boy	Washington, John	Capt Foretop
Smyth, Edward	Blacksmith	Weavings, James	Able Seaman

Webb, Edward	Ordinary Seaman	Wilson, Robert	Private
Wells, Noah	Able Seaman	Wittle, Herman	Able Seaman
Wells, William	Private	Woodford, John	Boy
West, Charles	Boy	Woodford, William H.	Boy
Westaway, Edwin	Bandsman	Woodford, William N.	Boy
Westcott, Robert	Ordinary Seaman	Woodley, John	Able Seaman
Wheeler, John	Private	Worsley, Edward	Leading Seaman
Whitbread, John	Cook's Mate	Wright, Joseph	Private
Whitcombe, Edward	Able Seaman	Wyatt, Henry H.	Secretary
White, Henry	Capt Maintop	Wyatt, John	Ordinary Seaman
White, John	Caulker	Young, Charles	Capt Foretop
Whittington, Henry	Able Seaman	Young, Tom	Krooman
Wigg, James	Sergeant (RM)		
Wilkins, Cornelius	Ward Room Off's Servant		
Will, Black	Krooman	*Returned Medals*	
William, King	Krooman	Andrews, Samuel	Ordinary Seaman
Williams, Alfred	Private	Astley, Evan	Ward Room Off's Servant
Williams, Henry	Gunner (RMA)	Barry, Thomas	Able Seaman
Duplicate medal issued		Bidgood, Noah	Boy
Williams, James	Able Seaman	Cain, John	Private
Williams, William G.	Gun Room Steward	France, Thomas	Private
Duplicate medal issued		Gready, William	Private
Williamson, George	Able Seaman	Legar, James	Ward Room Cook's Assistant
Willshire, Alfred	Able Seaman	Minty, James	Drummer
Wilson, Alfred	Sailmaker's Crew	Morrison, John	Private
Wilson, James	Able Seaman	Murphy, Michael	Private
Wilson, James	Private	Solomans, Frank	Bandsman
Wilson, Joe	Krooman	Staines, William	Gunner (RMA)

H.M.S. *Satellite*

Aboan	Captain's Cook	Blance, William	Able Seaman
Adams, John	Gunner (RMA)	Blaxham, George	Able Seaman
Ahern, John	Stoker	Bliss, William J.	Gunner
Ahern, William	Ordinary Seaman	Boden, Samuel	Acting Corporal
Aishton, Joseph	Capt Afterguard	Bolus, Alfred	Private
Alford, Joseph	Boy	Bonney, Edward T.	Quartermaster
Antonio, Joe	Ward Room Cook	Bourke, Southwell G. T.	Midshipman
Assing	Ward Room Off's Servant	Bowman, Henry J.	Lieutenant (RMLI)
Assong	Ward Room Off's Servant	Bradford, James	Boy
Assoon	Engineer's Cook	Bray, Robert P.	Caulker's Mate
Athing	Engineer's Servant	Brooks, John T.	Boy
Autridge, Rev F. C.	Chaplain & Naval Instr	Broome, John H.	Midshipman
Aze, Henry	Stoker	Brown, Patrick	Private
Bailey, Thomas	Boy	Brown, Thomas	Private
Ball, Walter	Ward Room Off's Servant	Brown, William J.	Ship's Steward Boy
Banks, Edward H.	Clerk	Bruce, Robert	Carpenter
Barry, Edmund	Able Seaman	Buckshought, George	Captain's Steward
Bates, William	Gunner (RMA)	Bunker, John	Stoker
Baynton, John C.	Pilot	Burt, Edmund W.	Sub Lieutenant
Bayton, Alfred	Stoker	Butland, Gilbert	Boy
Beare, John	Able Seaman	Capps, William F.	Chief Engineer
Beedle, Frank	Boy	Cardale, Charles S.	Senior Lieutenant
Bell, Charles	Stoker	Carter, Arthur T. S.	Midshipman
Bendell, Alfred	Private	Caunter, John F.	Boatswain's Mate
Billot, Philip A.	Ordinary Seaman	Chamberlain, William H.	Boy
Bishop, Edwin	Able Seaman	Chapman, George	Carpenter's Crew
Blake, Edwin	Ship's Corporal	Cheevers, William H.	Able Seaman

Child, James R.	Ship's Steward
Clancey, John	Able Seaman
Clark, John	Stoker
Clark, William J.	Stoker
Clements, John	Able Seaman
Clements, Robert	Capt Afterguard
Clements, William	Able Seaman
Close, William	Capt Maintop
Cole, Samuel	Carpenter's Mate
Collier, David	Private
Collings, Thomas	Able Seaman
Colter, Richard	Gunner's Mate
Cook, George F.	Able Seaman
Cook, Richard	Stoker
Cooper, John G.	Capt Maintop
Cosway, Henry	Boy
Courtney, Michael	Able Seaman
Cox, Samuel	Gunner (RMA)
Crawford, James	Engineer
Cross, Thomas	Engineer
Cuffley, Samuel	Private
Culbert, John	Able Seaman
Currie, John	Able Seaman
Daly, James	Capt Maintop
Darwin, Sacheverel C.	Lieutenant
Davies, Thomas	Ward Room Steward
Davis, Thomas	Gunner (RMA)
Davy, George	Boy
Davy, John	Boy
Dawson, John	Private
Desmond, Denis	Able Seaman
Dhue, Frederick	Leading Stoker
Dick, James M.	Surgeon
Donaher, James	Boy
Donoghue, Timothy	Boy
Downman, Richard D.	Boy
Driscoll, Daniel	Boy
Driscoll, Thomas	Shipwright
Drury, Edward	Leading Seaman
Dunne, Peter	Carpenter's Crew
Dunstan, John	Boy
Dwyer, John	Private
Edwards, William	Ordinary Seaman
Edye, Joseph	Captain
Elliott, George	Ship's Corporal
Ellis, Edward	Able Seaman
Evans, George S.	Ordinary Seaman
Fell, Iasiah E.	Signalman
Finn, Patrick	Able Seaman
Fitzgerald, Edward	Capt Afterguard
Fitzgerald, Patrick	Boy
Fletcher, Samuel	Able Seaman
Flynn, Edmund	Able Seaman
Franks, John	Blacksmith
Fry, George	Private
Fulton, William	Private
Gilbert, John	Boy
Gill, Charles F.	Able Seaman
Gittings, Robert	Ordinary Seaman
Glanville, John	Ordinary Seaman
Goodlake, William H. G.	Midshipman
Goulding, Thomas	Private
Gordon, Edward W.	Paymaster
Graham, James	Caulker
Grant, Robert	Cook's Mate
Greaves, Thomas E.	Coxwain Cutter
Greap, John	Able Seaman
Gregory, Joseph E.	Midshipman
Duplicate medal issued	
Griffiths, George	Sailmaker
Hadrill, Frederick	Drummer
Haggard, John G.	Midshipman
Hales, Thomas	Leading Stoker
Hall, Henry	Private
Hancock, William	Boatswain's Mate
Harding, John	Stoker
Harrigan, Michael	Private
Harrington, Michael	Able Seaman
Harris, Daniel	Able Seaman
Hartland, Joseph	Able Seaman
Haywood, Thomas	Private
Heath, Joseph	Private
Henderson, Thomas	Ordinary Seaman
Hicks, James	Leading Stoker
Hill, Edwin S.	Able Seaman
Hill, John G.	Capt Foretop
Hillings, Thomas	Boy
Hodge, George W.	Ordinary Seaman
Hodges, William	Sergeant
Holbrey, George	Corporal (RMA)
Horswell, Frederick	Boy
Hutchinson, Frederick	Midshipman
Irvine, George	Boy
Isaacs, Isaac	Lamptrimmer
Jenkins, Mathias	Capt Forecastle
Jennetts, John	Able Seaman
Jones, Cornwell	Able Seaman
Jones, William H.	Ordinary Seaman
Joynes, William	Private
Jukes, William A.	Act Sub Lieutenant
Kay, William H. F.	Clerk
Duplicate medal sent 17 August 1876	
Kearn, John	Ordinary Seaman
Kent, Edwin	Capt Mast
Kerrigan, Michael	Private
Kilbrow, Patrick	Stoker
Kirk, Edward J.	Private
Kitt, John	Able Seaman
Larkham, W. H.	Boy
Lawless, George	Act Paymaster
Lemon, Thomas	Able Seaman
Lewis, James	Leading Seaman
Libby, John E.	Boy
Liddle, Thomas	Ordinary Seaman

Lidstone, James	Ordinary Seaman
Limb, Charles	Sick Berth Attendant
Lindy, William	Captain's Coxwain
Lock, Henry B.	Ward Room Off's Servt
Lyons, Matthew	Able Seaman
McAnliffe, Patrick	Able Seaman
McCormick, John	Private
McDonald, John	Ordinary Seaman
McIntosh, Thomas	Asst Engineer
McKay, Jeremiah	Able Seaman
McMahon, James	Leading Seaman
Manley, Richard	Stoker
Marchant, William E.	Boy
Martin, John	Able Seaman
Martin, Nathanial	Cooper's Crew
Masters, Thomas	Able Seaman
Matthews, John	Leading Seaman
Matthews, Richard A.	Captain's Servant
Matthews, William	Acting Sergeant
Meade, Edward	Asst Surgeon
Medder, John	Warrant Officer's Cook
Mellish, John	Gun Room Cook
Merton, Thomas	Boy
Mills, George	Leading Seaman
Mitchell, James	Leading Seaman
Moore, George	Sailmaker's Crew
Morman, Robert	Ordinary Seaman
Mortimer, James	Private
Murphy, Patrick	Able Seaman
Musgrave, Philip	Midshipman
Munton, Leonard	Able Seaman
Newton, James	Stoker
Nodder, James	Capt Mast
O'Connell, John G.	Navigating Lieutenant
Oldfield, Henry J.	Act Lieutenant
Duplicate medal issued	
Osborne, Samuel L.	Lieutenant
Parker, Frederick	Sailmaker's Crew
Pavey, William	Boy
Pearce, John	Shipwright
Pennell, Frank	Gunner (RMA)
Penny, Thomas	Gunner (RMA)
Perkins, William	Gunner's Mate
Phillpotts, Arthur	Lieutenant
Pidgeon, James	Ship's Cook
Pierson, William	Stoker
Pitcher, Robert	Painter
Pitler, George	Blacksmith
Ponsford, William B.	Midshipman
Potter, John	Private
Pounds, Thomas	Quartermaster
Duplicate medal sent 5 November 1874	
Powell, Richmond F.	Midshipman
Prendergast, Michael	Boy
Prince, Edward B.	Able Seaman
Rainey, James	Ordinary Seaman
Raven, Frederick	Ordinary Seaman
Richard, E. P.	Able Seaman
Rickard, Nicholas J.	Ropemaker
Roach, Edward	Boatswain's Mate
Rosevere, Edward	Shipwright
Routledge, William	Private
Rowe, John	Carpenter's Crew
Rowley, George	Armourer
Russell, James	Ordinary Seaman
Ryall, Albert	Able Seaman
Saunders, John H.	Leading Stoker
Scoble, Robert J.	Leading Stoker
Sharpe, Thomas	Able Seaman
Shewell, William R.	Boy
Simmons, William H.	Ordinary Seaman
Simpson, William	Boatswain
Skiven, David	Capt Foretop
Spiller, George	Capt Maintop
Stancombe, Thomas	Stoker
Stanley, James	Able Seaman
Steer, Charles	Boy
Stephens, James	Tailor
Sullivan, John	Private
Sullivan, Thomas	Leading Seaman
Sweeny, David	Leading Seaman
Symons, John	Able Seaman
Symons, William	Ordinary Seaman
Tapprell, Reuben	Boy
Tate, Henry	Private
Teak, A.	Carpenter's Crew
Temple, William	Private
Townsend, William	Leading Seaman
Tracey, Patrick	Able Seaman
Tregenna, William	Gun Room Servant
Tregidgo, Jas R.	Ordinary Seaman
Tremayne, Charles F.	Master at Arms
Tucker, Alfred	Boy
Tucker, William	Leading Seaman
Turner, Joseph	Boy
Venn, William	Warrant Officer's Servant
Walker, James	Ordinary Seaman
Walker, Peter	Private
Walsh, James	Ordinary Seaman
Walsh, Richard	Able Seaman
Ward, Alfred	Capt Foretop
Warren, Charles	Gunner (RMA)
Duplicate medal issued	
Waters, John	Boy
Webb, Charles	Private
Webb, William P.	Boy
Wellington, William	Able Seaman
West, Richard	Quartermaster
Wigham, John	Private
Williams, Albert	Ward Room Off's Servant
Williams, Samuel	Capt Forecastle
Willis, Thomas	Ward Room Off's Servant
Winter, William	Ordinary Seaman
Wooding, William	Boy

Woodley, John H.	Boy	
Woodman, George	Able Seaman	
Woolner, George	Coxwain Launch	
Workman, George	Ordinary Seaman	
Wright, Robert	Boy	
Wright, Thomas	Able Seaman	
Wyatt, Arthur	Ordinary Seaman	
Yeo, Frederick	Carpenter's Crew	

Returned Medals

Aachie	Barber
Campbell, William	Private
Deary, Samuel	Boy
Foley, Donald	Able Seaman
Martin, Peter	Gunner (RMA)
Rollason, John	Ordinary Seaman
Walker, John	Able Seaman

H.M.S. *Spiteful*

Ariss, Robert	Private	Folley, William	Blacksmith's Mate
Barling, James	Cooper's Crew	Francis, Henry W.	2nd Capt Maintop
Bartlett, Samuel	Ward Room Steward	Frost, Henry	Boy
Bell, Richard	Ship's Corporal	Frost, James	Ordinary Seaman
Blackmore, William	Carpenter	Furneaux, Henry J.	Able Seaman
Bowen, Andrew	Abel Seaman	Goddard, Ira	Ordinary Seaman
Bradford, Jonathan	Stoker	Goldsmith, Jas W.	Carpenter's Crew
Bradshaw, Charles	Sick Berth Attendant	Gore, William J.	Ordinary Seaman
Brent, William	Able Seaman	Goulden, Henry	Ordinary Seaman
Bullen, George E.	Ordinary Seaman	Grant, Andrew	Yeoman Storeroom
Bulley, John	Painter	Groat, William	2nd Capt Afterguard
Burden, William	Able Seaman	Guppy, Robert W.	Able Seaman
Byrne, William	Lamptrimmer	Hall, James	Private
Cahill, Lawrence	Drummer (RM)	Hardy, George	Leading Seaman
Cardell, Louis	Engineer's Servant	Harry, James	Navigating Lieutenant
Carval, John	Gun Room Servant	Hart, Timothy	Leading Stoker
Chambers, Henry	Able Seaman	Hayworth, Richard	Private
Chappell, James H.	Quartermaster	Healey, Thomas	Stoker
Chenler, Edward	Private	Hearne, Elijah	Able Seaman
Clarke, James	Stoker	Hickey, Owen	Ordinary Seaman
Coghlan, Thomas	2nd Capt Maintop	Hill, John H.	Boy
Collins, Edwin C.	Boatswain	Hilston, Duncan	Surgeon
Collins, Thomas	Private	Hitchcock, George	Stoker
Connell, David	Boy	Hodge, Edwin	Boy
Cook, Francis	Private	Horton, Henry	Private
Cool, John	Stoker	Humphries, Thomas	Stoker
Cooper, Astley R.	Lieutenant	Hunt, William	Private
Courtney, Thomas	Stoker	Hurd, Reuben	Boy
Cotton, John	Ward Room Cook	Hussey, Joshua	Leading Stoker
Crump, Robert	Gunner	Hutchinson, Alfred	2nd Capt Afterguard
Darling, Henry G.	Gun Room Steward	James, Thomas W.	Ordinary Seaman
Day, Richard G.	Midshipman	Jenkins, William	Caulker
Deasy, Daniel	Sailmaker's Crew	Jennings, William	Ordinary Seaman
Donovan, Jeremiah	Boy	Jewell, Edward J.	Boy
Donovan, Michael	Boy	Jones, James	Boy
Downer, Charles	Gunner (RMA)	Jones, John	Captain's Cook
Driscoll, Thomas	Boy	Kingdom, George	Ordinary Seaman
Dungey, James T.	Ward Room Off's Servt	Lacey, James	Blacksmith
Dungey, William	Ward Room Off's Servt	Lamb, Henry	Private
Dyke, Henry H.	Act/Sub Lieutenant	Leeham, John	Stoker
Dyke, William	Stoker	Lefroy, Benjamin L.	Commander
Eddy, James R.	Boy	Legg, Richard	Quartermaster
Elgar, Alfred	Shipwright's Apprentice	Lenanghan, James	Private
Erridge, Robert G.	Ordinary Seaman	Letherick, Francis	Captain's Steward
Faulkner, Edward W. J.	Ship's Steward Boy	Lewis, Thomas O.	Chief Engineer
Findley, Joseph	Private	Linehane, Vincent	Boy

Lockie, Alfred	Leading Seaman
Littlefield, Augustus	Gunner's Mate
Longfield, William D.	Acting Surgeon
Lucas, Henry	Able Seaman
McCartey, John	Capt Forecastle
McDonald, Alfred L.	Able Seaman
McKenzie, Robert	Leading Seaman
Mackin, Isaac	Boy
Mansell, James C.	Boy
Marsh, Charles	Ordinary Seaman
Masterman, Henry	Asst Engineer
Matthews, Stephen	Engineer
Maudeville, Henry A.	Lieutenant
Miles, William	Ordinary Seaman
Mitchell, Samuel	Stoker
Moore, Henry J.	Ordinary Seaman
Moore, William H.	Able Seaman
Moores, Charles	Gunner
Morgan, Richard	Ward Room Off's Servt
Morton, Edward	Colour Sergeant (RMLI)
Mugeridge, John	Ordinary Seaman
Newland, James W.	Ordinary Seaman
Nicholson, William	Engineer
Nunn, George	Warrant Off's Cook
Oatley, George	Leading Seaman
Paine, Edwin	Armourer's Crew
Palmer, Benjamin	Stoker
Parrott, Edward	Captain's Coxwain
Payne, John	Engineer's Cook
Pearce, Alfred	Ordinary Seaman
Pearson, Arthur W.	Clerk
Pennicott, James	Carpenter's Mate
Pennington, James	Sailmaker's Mate
Penrose, Charles	Stoker
Perry, James	Able Seaman
Pike, James	Private
Pile, Walter	Able Seaman
Pippin, Samuel	Boy
Powell, William	2nd Capt Maintop
Price, William	Ordinary Seaman
Pyne, Charles E.	Midshipman
Reynolds, George	Shipwright
Reynolds, Philip M.	Carpenter's Crew
Richardson, Henry	Ordinary Seaman
Robbins, John	2nd Capt Foretop
Robins, George	Ordinary Seaman
Rogers, Francis R.	Ordinary Seaman
Roob, Adam	Private
Roper, Elijah	Gun Room Cook
Rumsey, Robert M.	Midshipman
Sanders, Richard	Ordinary Seaman
Searle, Joseph	Boy
Sermon, William	Ordinary Seaman
Sheldon, Stephen	Asst Engineer
Short, John	Able Seaman
Siggery, Thomas	Able Seaman
Simpkin, Thomas	Able Seaman
Skilton, Henry	Able Seaman
Smart, John	Stoker
Smith, James	Ordinary Seaman
Smith, James C.	Able Seaman
Smith, Richard	2nd Capt Foretop
Smith, Walter	Ward Room Off's Servant
Smith, William	Boatswain's Mate
Smith, William M. D.	Able Seaman
Stainer, William	Act/Navigating Sub Lieut
Stansfield, Thomas	Leading Stoker
Stevens, John	Stoker
Strickland, George	Capt Forecastle
Sueter, John T.	Paymaster
Taylor, George S.	Able Seaman
Ternan, Arthur O. R. B.	Midshipman
Tirzley, William L.	Stoker
Trundle, Charles E.	Able Seaman
Virgo, John	Ward Room Off's Servt
Ward, Thomas	Gunner

Duplicate medal sent 11 Nov 1873

Walker, Jonathan	Leading Stoker
Walsh, Patrick	2nd Capt Afterguard
Warren, Walter J.	Able Seaman
Whalley, William	Corporal (RMA)
Wheatly, John H.	Ordinary Seaman
Wickman, Joseph	Ordinary Seaman
Williams, Thomas	Warrant Off's Servant
Willmott, George	Signalman
Wilcox, John	Ship's Cook
Withell, William	Stoker
Woodrow, Frederick H.	Ship's Steward
Wright, William S.	Boy

Returned Medal

Southard, Charles	Boy

H.M.S. *Star*

Aitkin, Daniel	Leading Stoker
Antony, Thomas	Shipwright
Bailey, Joseph	Ship's Steward
Beer, John S.	Stoker
Bennett, John	Act Ship's Cook
Bennett, William R.	Surgeon
Blight, John	Able Seaman
Blight, Richard	Ship's Cook
Bohan, Daniel	2nd Capt Forecastle
Boobo, Tomby	Ward Room Steward
Bradshaw, Richard	Commander
Brimacombe, William	Asst Engineer
Bruce, John	Chief Engineer
Cameron, Verney L.	Lieutenant

Duplicate medal no 411 issued

Chamberlain, Robert	Private
Clifford, Henry	Able Seaman
Cook, James Henry	Ward Room Off's Servant

Coombe, William	2nd Capt Foretop	Marshall, Alfred	Gunner
Craig, William H.	Gunner	Mason, Samuel	Stoker
Crawley, Timothy	Stoker	Matthew, Matthew	Gunner
Cundy, William	Caulker's Mate	Millman, John	Ordinary Seaman
Davey, George	Able Seaman	Neagle, John	Quartermaster
Davis, John	Engineer's Servant	Nixdolf, Adolph	Able Seaman
Dollar, Tom	Krooman	Onions, John	Private
Drury, John	Asst Sick Berth Attn	O'Rourke, John	Able Seaman
Duffin, Hugh	Ordinary Seaman	Owen, John	Leading Stoker
Elliott, William	Leading Stoker	Oxland, Benjamin	Able Seaman
Evans, Thomas	Ordinary Seaman	Paramoe	Captain's Steward
Finnie, Alexander	Quartermaster	Pardon, John	Sergeant (RMLI)
Foster, Emanuel	Leading Seaman	Parsons, William	Stoker
Gale, John	Private	Payton, Francis	Krooman
George, Frederick	Warrant Off's Cook	Peter, John	2nd Head Krooman
George, James	Able Seaman	Pomeroy, James	Boy
George, King	Krooman	*Duplicate medal issued*	
Goddard, Samuel S.	Able Seaman	Potham, Henry E.	Ward Room Off's Servant
Greig, Octavius	Midshipman	Prince, George	Captain's Coxwain
Gundry, William	Able Seaman	Pryn, William	Able Seaman
Hannigan, Arthur	Private	Pullee, Sanligo	Captain's Cook
alias McCormick		Pulli, Serampara	Ward Room Cook
Duplicate medal sent 17 July 1884		Richards, Thomas	Able Seaman
Haswell, William H.	Paymaster	Rider, Henry	Act Engineer
Hayles, George	Acting Gunner	Rogers, John E.	Able Seaman
Hennessey, David	Ordinary Seaman	Sands, James	Private
Hickson, Thomas	Gunner	Smith, Alexander	Sailmaker's Mate
Hill, Charles	Stoker	Snell, John S.	Navigating Lieutenant
Hill, James G.	Engineer	Sweeney, Daniel	Boy
Holwell, Samuel	Stoker	Sweetman, Samuel	Stoker
Jekyll, Joseph W. L.	Lieutenant	Swift, John	Private
Johnson, Jacob	Krooman	Tilley, James	Private
Jones, James	Act Bombardier	Travers, William	Stoker
Kenefick, John	Ordinary Seaman	Twoglass, Tom	Krooman
Ker, D. Charles	Clerk	Viney, George	Gunner
Kicks, John	Gunner	Walsh, Maurice	Boy
Knott, John	Boatswain's Mate	Webb, William H. G.	Asst Engineer
Lane, William H.	Private	West, Joseph	Stoker
Lewes, Jack	Krooman	Wiles, Benjamin	Ordinary Seaman
Lewis, Charles R.	Chief Carpenter's Mate	Will, Frederick	Gunner's Mate
Littleton, Simon T.	2nd Capt Maintop	Williams, George J.	Leading Seaman
Liverpool, Ben	Head Krooman	Wood, William	Stoker
Lovatt, Thomas	Boy		
Lynch, John G.	Boatswain	*Returned Medal*	
McKeer, George	Stoker	Stillwell, James	Stoker

H.M.S. *Vigilant*

Ahing	Caulker's Mate	Body, Henry W.	Ordinary Seaman
Amis, Spiro	Krooman	Brockman, Charles B. L.	Paymaster
Bainbridge, Jno H.	Senior Lieutenant	Brown, Ralph A. O.	Commander
Baker, J. W.	Private	Bull, William	Leading Stoker
Barker, William R.	Ordinary Seaman	Camp, Albert	Boy
Barrett, Richard	Ship's Cook	Campbell, George	Leading Stoker
Bastian, Sendia	Ward Room Off's Servant	Carlie, Veerufron	Ward Room Cook
Beadle, Frederick	Boy	Chappel, George	Ordinary Seaman
Bicknell, William J.	Ordinary Seaman	Chase, William	Leading Stoker
Bishop, John	Private	Clifton, John	Ordinary Seaman

Condun, S.	Captain's Cook
Constant, William	Boy
Coomber, Robert	Sergeant RM
Cornick, Joshua P.	2nd Capt Forecastle
Cornish, George S.	Asst Engineer
Cowley, Joseph	Leading Seaman
Cryer, William	Asst Sick Berth Attendant
Curtin, Patrick	Ordinary Seaman
Darby, John R.	Chief Carpenter's Mate
Dennis, Jas C. C.	Lieutenant
Drinan, David	Ordinary Seaman
English, John	Private
Fernandes, Luis	Musician
Folkes, Henry	Boy
Foster, William J.	Engineer
Frazer, Thomas R.	Gunner (RMA)
Gambling, Robert	Ordinary Seaman
Gray, John	Ordinary Seaman
Grose, William H.	Engineer
Hall, Edward T.	Ordinary Seaman
Henderson, Jas E.	Boy
Henslow, Henry	Leading Stoker
Hine, Thomas	Boatswain
Hosford, Thomas	Sailmaker's Mate

Duplicate medal sent 1 June 1876

Howie, James	Blacksmith
Hughes, Henry	Private
Hutchinson, Daniel	Private
Jackson, Albert	Quartermaster
Jackson, Gordon	Surgeon
Jones, James	Ward Room Off's Servant
Jumbo, James	Stoker
Kelly, Murty	Private
Kent, James	Private
Kilby, William	Captain's Coxwain
King, Edward W.	Able Seaman
Kingscott, Henry	Gunner (RMA)
Kyte, John	Private
Lamb, Smith	Bombardier (RMA)
Lane, William J.	Carpenter's Crew
Lazarus, Vestiam	Ward Room Off's Servant
Lock, George	Warrant Officer's Cook
Long, George J.	Clerk
McAvoy, Edward	Chief Engineer
Maguire, David	Ordinary Seaman

Duplicate medal sent 17 May 1876

Mason, William	Stoker
Meadows, Arthur	Ship's Steward
Mitchell, William	Gunner (RMA)
Mootto, Tamby	Captain's Steward
Pemberry, William J.	Stoker
Pepper, Tom	Head Krooman
Phipps, Richard	Stoker
Rice, George	Stoker
Rimmer, James	Boy
Robinson, William	Gunner (RMA)
Rosever, William J.	Boy
Sears, William	Quartermaster
Shepherd, Edward	Stoker
Siger, John	Shipwright
Singleton, Thomas	Blacksmith
Sinnatamby, Tombaya	Captain's Cook's Asst
Smith, Henry	Navigating Lieutenant
Smith, John	2nd Capt Foretop
Smith, Jno R.	Gunner (RMA)
Spiro, Arris	Krooman
Tull, Frederick	Gunner's Mate
Upchurch, Joseph	Ordinary Seaman
Warne, Jas R.	Boatswain's Mate
Warne, William	2nd Capt Maintop
Warrington, Albert T. C.	Lieutenant
West, Frederick	Ordinary Seaman
Whincap, Jas N.	Stoker
White, Charles R.	Boy
Williams, Frank	Ordinary Seaman
Wilson, Robert	Ordinary Seaman
Wood, Walter	Ordinary Seaman
Wright, Robert	Leading Seaman
Young, George	Ward Room Steward

Returned Medals

Bailey, Ephraim	Able Seaman
Gwyer, Charles	Engineer's Servant
Keenan, Peter	Gunner

Discharged the Service by Court Martial

Kenny, William	Able Seaman

Discharged the service as objectionable

Madden, Martin	Stoker
Matthews, Alfred E.	Stoker
Woodley, Charles	Leading Seaman